CITY–CHANGING PRAYER

When Debra and Frank Green speak, it's with a quiet anointing and authority that comes from years of effective, relational Christian leadership. God is using them to build his church in Manchester through city-wide prayer and real friendships. They are leaders with integrity, passion and a proven track record. They are also good fun! I cannot commend them highly enough.

Pete Greig – 24/7 Prayer

Jesus prayed that we may be united in him. We've seen in Greater Manchester that when Christians act together and base their action on united prayer then God uses them to bless the City. We enter into partnership with people of all faiths and none – for the good of our communities – and 'we bring God with us!'

Rt Revd David Gillett, Bishop of Bolton

Frank and Debra have worked tirelessly and passionately to bring about the co-operation of churches in prayer and inter-cession for our city. Their work has brought about a momentum that continues to be seen today in our respective communities.

Paul and Mags Hallam, Senior Pastors, Lighthouse Christian Centre (Elim Pentecostal), Manchester

The journey God has been taking his people on in Manchester has been exciting, messy and glorious. In many ways it has only just begun but I am convinced we would not be where we are today without the undergirding of an area wide, mission focused, groundswell of prayer. Read this book; it will get you on your knees and then things can really start to happen.

Roger Sutton, Senior Pastor, Altrincham Baptist Church

There are two things above everything else that bring churches together to impact entire communities – God-honouring prayer and God-filled personalities. For over a decade Frank and Debra Green have sought to incarnate and demonstrate both of these in Manchester. We owe them an enormous debt for their inspiration and example.

Chick Yuill, Salvation Army

It has been so rewarding for me as a Christian police officer to be able to work with Frank and Debra over the last few years as they have encouraged churches to work together in local areas alongside the police and civic authorities with the aim of seeing communities transformed, crime reduced and the lives of individuals changed by a living personal faith.

Supt Alison Fletcher, Greater Manchester Police

City-Changing Prayer

DEBRA AND FRANK GREEN

survivor

Unless otherwise indicated, biblical quotations are from
the New International Version © 1973, 1978, 1984
by the International Bible Society.
Quotations from the Good News Bible
© American Bible Society 1976, published by the Bible Society and
HarperCollins.

ISBN 1 84291 218 6

Survivor is an imprint of KINGSWAY COMMUNICATIONS LTD
Lottbridge Drove, Eastbourne, BN23 6NT, England.
Email: books@kingsway.co.uk

Printed in the USA

To Sarah, Becky, Josh and Matthew

Acknowledgements

There are literally hundreds of people who deserve recognition for the part they have played, and in many cases still do play, in changing Manchester and the surrounding areas through prayer and action. Some of them are listed here as a token of our appreciation and to acknowledge the privilege it is for us to be able to work with them for God's glory.

Yaw Adudwamaa, Cliff Allchin, Wendy and Mark Ashcroft, Hannah Atkins, David Baker, Colin Barron, Matt Beemer, Estar Bennett, Jason Bent, Eric Berrisford, Paul Booth, Sharon and Andy Britton, Ian Cameron, Muriel Chad, Sandra and Simon Chadwick, Mike Chesterton, Jerry Clifford, David Corke, Owen Crane, Oria Dale, Graham Deakin, Peter Dearden, Alph Dormekpor, Debbie Edwards, Alison Fletcher, Keith Garner, Ross Garner, Ben Gilchrist, David Gillett, Kim and Adrian Glasspole, Phil Gleave, Becky Green, Sarah Green, Jean and Ken Hall, Paul Hallam, Colin Hardicre, Michael Harvey, Michelle and Andy Hawthorne, Phil Hobrough, Marijke Hoek, Paul Keeble, Jackie Marsh, Rhona Marshall, Christopher Mayfield, Alan Morton, Arnold Muwonge, Adrian Nottingham, John Owen, Gordon and Lorna Pettie, Sarah Phillips, Andy Poole, June

Richards, Carl Roach, Annabel Roberts, Julia Robertson, Ian Rowbottom, Rob Ruston, Val Sillavan, Sue Sinclair, Lucy and Andi Smith, Debbie and Chris Summerton, Roger Sutton, Lynn Swart, Ann Taylor, Robert Varnam, Chris Vedder, Neil Wain, Paul Wenham, Joy Wright, Simon Wrigley, Cyprian Yobera, Margaret and Chick Yuill.

Bolton: Martin Bullivant, Rob Coleman, Mark Curtis, Lik-Kee McKaine, Derek Smith.

Bury: Rod Fairbrother, David Malloy, Bruce Millar, David Milner.

Oldham: John Brocklehurst, Doug Clarke, Steve Cowling, Andrew Davies, Terry Durose, Graham Horsley, Graham Radcliffe

Preston: Pam and Arnold Cooke, Graham Hooke, Andy Prosser.

Rochdale: Ron Cave, David Corke, Jan Smith, Alan Reeve.

Rossendale: Stephen Duffy, Neil Hepworth.

Salford: Lee Hardy, Pat Howarth, David King, Malcolm Lane, Mike Saunders.

Stockport: Jeannie Birtwistle, Paul Booth, Steve Bullock, Pauline Lucas, Dave Martin, Austin Moore, Philip Wilcoxon, Phil Winn.

Tameside: Tony Higginson, Gareth Lloyd-Jones, Ray Shepherd.

Trafford: John Beaney, Rob Cannon, Steve Cockram, Jez Green, Andrew Hardcastle, Phil Rawlings.

Wigan: Marjorie Ellis, Lynn Fowler, Jan Harney.

Contents

Foreword

Frank and Debra Green really are two of my favourite people not just because they are my friends and I enjoy their company but because I believe their ministry has been absolutely key in anything we have been able to achieve through The Message Trust over these last few years.

In my heart, when we started the trust I knew that the real breakthroughs would only come if we stepped up the prayer for this city, and that if good things were to happen in the schools or on the estates it would only be as part of the mopping up operation – the real battle would be won in the heavenlies. However, as an evangelist and an activist, I have to confess that the thought of endless hours of interceding rather than getting out there proclaiming the message didn't fill me with enthusiasm. We've always tried to build our team life around regular times of prayer and fasting but still I know that without the faithful support of so many, and in particular Debra and Frank, none of the growth and impact we've seen in this tough northern city would have been possible.

On the wall of my office I have a framed pair of scissors that someone gave me after one of our events. On one blade is written 'evangelism' and on the other 'prayer'. Underneath it reads 'Andy – keep on the cutting edge.' It's only through the two combined activities that we're going to cut through. Prayer without mission can so easily become self-centred; mission without prayer is always powerless.

The evangelism we've engaged in over recent years has been increasingly 'word and deed', yet all the acts of kindness in the world simply won't get the job done without faithful, sacrificial prayer. That's why it's such a joy to endorse this timely book. Frank and Debra are the real deal, and the prayer movement they've pioneered in Manchester, with the poor and the lost right at the heart, is now being replicated in many other towns and cities across the UK.

Whatever you do, though, don't just read this book. Catch the fire and see your city changed by the most powerful force in the universe – united, sacrificial prayer.

Andy Hawthorne

introduction
it all begins with prayer

Frank

A book about prayer

This is a book about prayer. But it's not about personal prayer. It's about how God is calling Christians from different denominations and streams to pray together for their towns and cities in a way that will bring about social transformation. It's about the kind of prayer that arises from hearts of agreement across traditional dividing lines. It's about prayer that attracts the attention of Almighty God because its agenda is in line with his. Prayer that connects with the needs and challenges of Western urban society in the twenty-first century. Prayer that leads to action and causes things and people to change: city-changing prayer.

God loves the towns and cities of our nation, but he hates the mess they're in. And in these days, with urban populations hitting record levels, he's calling the church more loudly and clearly than ever before to co-operate in prayer and action to begin to turn things around for his glory. The church is God's primary agent of change on earth and while we might not agree completely with John Wesley, who said that 'God does nothing except in answer to prayer', we only need cast a cursory glance across the great Christian revivals of church history to remind ourselves that they all began in prayer and led to major social reform. Sadly, in between those mighty moves of God, the church has tended to lose its cutting edge and revert to general introspection. Although evangelicals have kept some form of outward focus alive by emphasising gospel proclamation, we too have largely failed to make much impact on society.

Thankfully, though, God loves his world too much to allow his church to fall asleep completely, and over the last 20 years or so evangelicals have embraced an important but previously overlooked truth about what it means to make Christ known to the world around us. We have begun to rediscover the social implications of personal faith. The 'personal saviour' theology of the mid to late twentieth century is giving way to a more biblically balanced view of the Christian's broader role in the redemptive plan of God. Faith is certainly personal but salvation is now perceived as a wider concept than merely an individual's ticket to eternal bliss. Individual salvation is increasingly being understood as a component part of God's grandiose plan of bringing everything to wholeness in Christ; perhaps 'cosmic saviour' theology would be a more appropriate term. When we begin to view our salvation as part of this wider picture, we realise that conversion brings with it social responsibility as well as personal benefit. Believers are saved to serve.

Caring about and for the human needs of people is now recognised as a core component of evangelism by most Bible-believing Christians. The days are fast disappearing when social action was considered a distraction from the primary task of proclaiming the Word. The current challenge facing Christians is to pool our spiritual resources and work together across denominations and streams for social transformation, espe-

16

cially in the towns and cities of our nation where the manifesta-
tions of evil are increasing at an even greater rate than the
growth in population. We need to hear again the ancient
charge:

> If my people, who are called by my name, will humble themselves
> and pray and seek my face and turn from their wicked ways; then
> will I hear from heaven and will forgive their sin and will heal their
> land. (2 Chronicles 7:14)

We are his people. Those of us who name Christ as Lord and
Saviour are members of his body on earth – God's main means
of redeeming and renewing his glorious creation, soiled and
spoiled as it is by the effects of human rebellion against his rule.

Because he has invested himself in his creation and paid the
supreme price for its transformation, we can be confident that
God will not wash his hands of the whole thing. He is not just
upholding all things by his powerful word (Hebrews 1:3) but
also making everything new (Revelation 21:5) and bringing all
things to reconciliation through Christ (Colossians 1:20). From
the moment of Christ's miraculous conception in Mary's womb,
the Holy Spirit has been fully employed on earth cleaning up
the cosmos and furthering the Father's long-term plan to renew
the universe.

We need to find realistic and practical ways of responding to
this challenge from the book of Chronicles which reaches us
still from thousands of years ago, so that we can begin to
experience the healing of the land that's become so urgent in
our time. To do so, we'll need to ask some foundational
questions like:

- What exactly does it mean to be the 'people of God' in a
  city?

- How can we demonstrate repentance, and what are our 'evil ways'?

- How much humility is enough, and what does it look like?

- How do we seek God's face for the needs of our town?

Prayer Network

In the early 1990s, God spoke clearly to Debra and myself about getting Christians in Manchester together to pray for the city. We followed his nudges and promptings and began to see very clearly an emerging city-wide vision for inter-church prayer and action. Now, some ten years or so later, we're reflecting on our experience and offering some insights that we hope will be useful in other places. It seems reasonable to assume that most areas will face similar challenges when it comes to getting churches together. There are likely to be memories of past hurts, unresolved disagreements, doctrinal differences, suspicion and cynicism, apathy and possibly a general lack of confidence in God's ability to overcome these obstacles.

We've been very privileged in Manchester to see the beginnings of some real breakthroughs in all these barriers to blessing. After a decade or so, people are at last starting to trust and respect one another across the denominational boundaries, and genuine, enthusiastic co-operation in mission is happening with increasing frequency and ease. It all began with prayer.

Humility and repentance are no longer just concepts to discuss but are now becoming visible realities in the developing relationships between believers of different traditions. We're also beginning to see the early shoots of social transformation, much of which can be directly linked to the new partnerships that are emerging between churches, mission agencies and secular authorities. And it all began with prayer.

Prayer changes things; at least, that's what Christians have always said. Why, then, are we surprised when we see the evidence?

Mobilising the majority

From the very start of Prayer Network we always tried to be focused and intentional about what we were doing. God was calling Christians to pray – not just intercessors but Christians in general across the board. The call was to pray for the city, not just for churchy stuff but for the very fabric of the city, its life, health and prosperity. We sensed a call to gather people together across church boundary lines, recognising and celebrating differences yet uniting in a common goal: to pray for spiritual breakthrough.

So we pray for the city council, for the police, for schools, for young people, for race relations, for business, for the arts and so on. We ask the Lord to act for his glory and for the benefit of the city. Praise God that we're already able to see and to celebrate some of his answers! Our prayer gatherings sometimes involve thousands, usually take place in large venues, and always include believers from just about every tradition and background (and often some non-believers too).

In themselves, these gatherings provide opportunities for Christians to learn from each other different ways of praying and worshipping. Charismatics discover that quiet reflection in a large gathering can lead to as much of a power encounter with the Holy Spirit as an upbeat session of high praise; Traditionalists find that singing new songs with rock rhythms can be just as uplifting as some of the best old hymns. We're all learning to respect and rejoice over the variety of churchmanship that exists within the body of Christ. More importantly, though, we're learning to open up our thoughts to what God wants to change in our society and to open our hearts to let his Spirit begin to stir and mould us into the agents of God's kingdom that we're called to be. Prayer is a powerful first step in the transformation of towns and cities.

Why this book?

The purpose of this book is twofold: first, to trace and track the development of what has grown over the years into a fruitful and inspiring prayer movement in our city; second, to encourage Christians in other places to start similar networks of prayer as a first step towards the kind of social transformation we've all read about in our history books.

We've reflected on how we heard from God and tried to be faithful in following his agenda. We've analysed the structures and strategies we employed along the way and tried to identify transportable principles that we're confident will work in most settings. In addition, we've endeavoured to be brave enough to ask tough questions, despite not always having the answers.

The two of us have always worked together in our attempts to stimulate city-changing prayer in Manchester, but Debra has always led the way in terms of vision and direction. Along with others, I play my part in supporting her and using my own gifts as a member of her team. We've worked together, too, in the writing of this book, although Debra has graciously allowed my editorial influence throughout. We offer it in the sincere hope that you'll be blessed and encouraged, maybe even inspired by what you read.

one

a heart for the city

Debra

The call

Frank and I sensed the earliest stirrings of a call to full-time ministry at a Spring Harvest type event way back in the early 1980s. The holiday/Bible week in question was actually called Filey Week. It was run by MWE (Movement for World Evangelisation), and the people we remember most from it are Dave Pope, Doug Barnett and Gilbert Kirby.

It was our first experience of heaven on earth! People of all ages, from a variety of backgrounds sharing life together on the edge of the Arctic Circle with nothing more than the cardboard walls of a chalet or the flapping canvas of a marquee to shield us from the bracing weather of the north-east coast of England.

The fellowship, though, was warm and we enjoyed the rich diet of teaching, worship and intense discussion over late-night refreshments. When the week was over we came home on a spiritual high, our hearts refreshed by the blessing of mixing with so many godly people from so many different types of church. Our heads were crammed full of truth, and our spirits stirred by a clear call to begin to prepare for what was then called 'The Ministry'.

We were embarrassed about this because we'd only been Christians for a couple of years and felt as though we shouldn't even be allowing our thoughts to wander in this direction. Surely every Christian aspired to be a pastor, evangelist or missionary – were we trying to push in ahead of those who were far more qualified and worthy? Because of this we kept quiet and simply got stuck in to as many aspects of church life as we could, while devouring the Bible, commentaries, testimony books and so on.

A few years later, we shared our sense of calling with our leaders. They encouraged us to apply to Bible college and embark on a period of training. The details of the next five years are another story entirely. Suffice it to say that God graciously provided for all our needs, including three years of on-the-job training at Altrincham Baptist Church. This ran in parallel with Frank's theological studies – by far the best model of training, according to him.

Next, we had to find a church that would take us on. This took a year, and involved some fascinating new experiences like 'preaching with a view' and 'ministerial search committees' – not particularly edifying for the ones doing the 'candidating'.

There were some pretty low moments during that year, when we wondered if we were on the wrong track completely. We prayed and listened to God, always making sure that we were open to the leading of the Holy Spirit about where we should move to. One particular friend challenged us about whether we would be willing to go overseas – he had a thing about France, and always tried his best to persuade Christians to go there as missionaries. The prospect of this horrified us but we wanted to be submissive and so added this to the list of possibilities, which at that stage included Watford, Cambridge, Birkenhead and Chester.

Spiritual home

All the opportunities we considered seemed wrong for one reason or another, and by 1991 we were a family of five under pressure to find stability. We told God that we would go anywhere in the world – even France, if that was his will!

Looking back, we often wonder if that was some sort of test that we finally passed. God seemed to enjoy opening a door for us at Ivy Cottage Church in Didsbury, Manchester, just five miles away from where we lived in north Cheshire!

Everything fell into place perfectly. We didn't even need to move house immediately, let alone learn a new language! Our new spiritual home was lively; it was led by a wise and godly pastor who had worked faithfully for unity in the city for years, Richard Harbour, who frequently challenged the congregation to develop the same kind of heart for Manchester that God had given him.

At first, we were too busy to take much notice of this. However, before long Frank and I both began to realise that we didn't have to develop a heart for the city – we already had one. Two, actually! Both of us were born in Manchester, and, apart from each spending a few years of our childhood in such foreign parts as Bromley (me) and Newcastle (Frank), we had lived here all of our lives. Manchester was our home.

The intriguing thing is that neither of us was aware of how important our city was to us until we found ourselves in this new environment. We did move house – a distance of only four miles but a significant crossing of the city limits and a change of postcode that somehow put us in touch with a sense of rootedness and belonging that had lain dormant within both of us.

It wasn't easy to move closer into the city; our cosy, suburban lifestyle was extremely comfortable – we loved the leafy lanes, and our children played safely with their well-mannered friends; the local schools were centres of excellence in every sense; insurance premiums were low; neighbours were polite, and even the dogs seemed to understand the importance of keeping the pavements clean. However, despite the upheaval, we soon felt at home in every way, and very quickly sensed God's leading to begin to demonstrate our passion for the city in a tangible way.

We began to realise that we took our city for granted. We enjoyed all its benefits – the shops, concert venues, restaurants, sporting facilities, employment opportunities and so on – but it never once occurred to us that we ought consciously to appreciate this. Like so many, we took all the city had to offer and never considered giving anything back. After all, didn't the city exist for the benefit of its inhabitants (especially those fortunate enough to inhabit its more comfortable fringe)?

In retrospect, we now realise that God was raising the subject of cities and their significance in the consciousness of many of his people at that time. We found ourselves reading articles and books about God's concern for cities and his desire to reverse the social problems that were so common in urban settings all around the world. Our paths began to cross with people like Roger and Faith Forster, Gerald Coates and others who were organising city-wide prayer initiatives, believing that the first steps to addressing these issues for God must be taken in prayerful unity throughout the body of Christ.

City life

Our burden for Manchester grew as we researched and discovered the great significance of our city, not only in its present-day contribution to music, fashion and sport but also historically in the Industrial Revolution, the IT industry, the trade union movement, the co-operative movement and so on.

And yet, for all its industry and pioneering creativity, our research made us keenly aware of the fact that Manchester is a split city. The north–south divide is strikingly evident, with property prices the clearest indicator – houses in south Manchester are generally worth twice what they are in the north. Most factories and warehouses are in the north, and yet almost all their owners live in the south. There is an unspoken yet very real antipathy between the residents of north and south Manchester.

School league tables are another indicator, with some south Manchester schools featuring among the nation's best, while some north Manchester schools languish near the very bottom. In 2004, one area of north Manchester, Harpurhey, was identified as the worst place to live in the whole of the UK. Certain areas of south Manchester feature among the list of the nation's most desirable – with footballers, TV stars and pop singers driving their Ferraris and Range Rovers through the leafy lanes.

Racial divisions are evident throughout the city, with certain areas totally ghettoised. Rusholme, for example, is an urban village on the edge of the city centre with so many Asian restaurants along both sides of its High Street that it's nicknamed Curry Mile. Nearby, Moss Side and Longsight are notorious centres of drug trafficking and shootings. The majority of residents are black. Some schools are made up almost

25

entirely of black and Asian pupils; others are almost exclusively white.

Like most major cities, Manchester suffers a high incidence of crime. The statistics predictably vary according to area, with the poorer inner-city areas and pockets of urban estates scattered around the suburbs experiencing crime rates of well above the national average.

As they do in all parts of the world, young people divide themselves along the lines of football allegiance (City or United, in case you weren't sure!), dress codes, musical preferences and so on. In a city like ours, all of these are heightened by the sheer volume of youngsters and the ready availability of negative role models, cheap drugs and stealable property. Gangs hang around every street corner, and shopping centres feel unsafe in daylight as well as after dark.

Like city, like church?

Historically, the church in Manchester has failed to make much impact either socially or in terms of conversions: church attendance averages out at lower than 5 per cent of the population, less than half the national average.

Worse, maybe, is the unnerving observation that the church appears to reflect the city in terms of its disunity and fragmentation. Unlike most major UK towns and cities, Manchester has never experienced a significant Christian revival. In the eighteenth century, John Wesley's ministry yielded little fruit in our city. Although a Methodist central hall was eventually built in the centre, the numbers of conversions during his visits were uncharacteristically low.

In the 1960s, Billy Graham's rallies at Maine Road, the then home of Manchester City FC, were certainly successful but not on the same scale as those held at Haringey in London.

According to anecdotal evidence, in his one visit to the UK in 1873, the American evangelist D.L. Moody encountered a lack of unity between church leaders only in the city of Manchester. In Sunderland, Newcastle, Sheffield, Birmingham, Liverpool and throughout Scotland huge crowds of over 10,000 people flocked to hear him, and the meetings were characterised by great joy and Christian fervour. In Manchester, however, although a degree of practical success was recorded in terms of social work, there was little evidence of any significant spiritual renewal.

More recently, there had been division and antagonism between church leaders for the last 20 years, with different groups vying for recognition as the definitive body to authorise city-wide Christian activities. There was one group that had been so influential throughout the 1970s and 1980s that it was unofficially referred to as 'The Manchester Mafia'. Rumour has it that no large Christian event of any sort had been able to take place in the city without its approval, although its members were now ageing rapidly and a new generation of younger leaders was emerging.

Thankfully, we were blissfully unaware of these facts when, in 1992, we began to sense God calling us to start a city-wide prayer initiative. In our naivety, we imagined that if God was speaking then everyone would listen and want to respond with great enthusiasm. We had never even heard of church politics in those days, and never thought for one minute that our attempts to organise something that gathered Christians from different churches might be perceived in a negative light in some quarters.

27

Dreams and visions

To begin with, all we did was talk to each other about how good it would be to have a regular, inter-church prayer meeting with a specific city focus. We were two people with a dream that we hoped would one day materialise. We had no plans, nor even the faintest idea of what would be needed to make it happen. Our lives were busy, with our family and local church responsibilities taking up all our available time. There didn't seem to be any way we could take on something else.

But we did make time to pray, and gradually sensed that God was so concerned about our city that he wanted us to be willing to let him take our dream to the next level. It seemed clear to us that we had inadvertently hit upon something that was very important to God. I remember years ago hearing a preacher challenging Christians to 'find out what's breaking God's heart and let it break yours too'. Without actually setting out to do this, we found ourselves in exactly that position. The condition of our city was breaking God's heart, and he was calling his people to do something about it.

As the two of us prayed together over the next few months, we began to 'see' Manchester in the spiritual realm. God was revealing to us a picture of how things appeared from his point of view: Manchester appeared in the form of an ancient city surrounded by fortified walls. The original layout could be seen clearly but the walls were broken down in many places, leaving gaping holes through which enemy armies were riding to plunder the resources of the city and spoil the lives of its inhabitants. Standing among the remains of the walls were several towers. They seemed to be strong and secure, and were places of refuge for some of the people.

Our interpretation of the picture was that the strong towers symbolised churches that resisted the enemy. They were dotted about all around the city. Some were large, others small, but all of them seemed strong; this, to us, spoke of their faithfulness to the Lord and his kingdom. But they had become isolated from each other and, although they were strong in themselves, their distance from one another was allowing the devil to wreak havoc all around them. We sensed a clear challenge from God to call these strong towers to an awareness of this reality and to enable ways of rebuilding the broken walls in order to enable communication and relationship between them, so strengthening the city's spiritual defences.

As we prayed further into this vision, God showed us a glimpse of the future: as the walls began to rise in the picture, other towers appeared within the city; these represented new works of the kingdom that would eventually be established to bring blessing to the people and glory to the King.

City agenda

Looking for guidance from the Bible, we found ourselves drawn repeatedly to the Old Testament book of Nehemiah and, as we studied it, God showed us how Manchester was suffering the effects of a spiritual destruction that paralleled the physical devastation of post-exilic Jerusalem. Set in the fifth century BC, the book of Nehemiah recounts how God inspired his people to restore the derelict defences of their city.

Since the destruction of Jerusalem by the Babylonians in 586 BC, only a small number of Jews had lived there, among the ruins, eking out an existence as best they could. Their numbers began to increase in 538 BC when King Cyrus of Persia (who had conquered the Babylonians and now ruled the known world) authorised the start of a Temple reconstruction project. Cyrus took a different approach to controlling conquered nations, preferring to delegate authority to trustworthy governors and encouraging exiles to return and regenerate their economies rather than keeping them in captivity somewhere else. He even sponsored this project financially and returned many items of Temple furniture that had been plundered by the Babylonians 50 years previously.

Thousands of exiled Jews returned to their former capital and began the ambitious task of restoring the Temple. They faced hostile opposition from the people of the surrounding areas, who saw the project as a major threat to their own social and political stability. In total, it took almost 80 years to complete the task, and even then the finished product was a mere shadow of its glorious predecessor.

Although many houses had been rebuilt by the returning exiles, the city walls had been left in ruins. The once proud city of God, admired and envied by the rulers of the nations, still languished in a state of unkempt neglect, a symbol of the faithlessness and disobedience of Israel. Successive generations had grown so accustomed to living among the rubble that they had lost sight of any possibility of things improving.

Regeneration

In his mercy, and in line with his plans to transform his creation through the lives and witness of his people, God called Nehemiah to lead the way in rebuilding the walls of Jerusalem. This would be a powerful first step towards repairing the infrastructure of the city. Once the place was defended again and its occupants united around the common goal of glorifying their God, then endless possibilities for social and spiritual renewal would emerge.

The task was huge; the people lacked motivation and looked only to their individual agendas and interests. Archaeologists have discovered evidence that, prior to Nehemiah's arrival, the only building work that had been carried out in Jerusalem was on individual homes. There seemed to be no sense of community and no corporate identity. On top of this, the opposition was substantial: Jerusalem was surrounded by a number of nations all united in their hatred of the Jews.

We realised that local churches and mission agencies in Manchester were guilty of a similar self-focused outlook; this was also true of many individual Christians. In fact, we were convicted ourselves of this very point. Did we really care about the spiritual state our city was in? What had we ever done to promote change regarding the many obvious social problems? Weren't we equally caught up with our own localised and inward-looking issues? What kind of collective expression of the church did we contribute to in our own area? The broken-down walls of Jerusalem spoke volumes to us as we considered Manchester's spiritual condition.

Taking our inspiration from Nehemiah himself, we set about analysing the spiritual condition of our city. Nehemiah assessed the situation by walking around and seeing the devastation of the walls of Jerusalem for himself. We walked the streets of Manchester and drove around them in the car, asking God for spiritual eyes to see things as he saw them.

The picture grew clearer and clearer. Physically, our city had a lot in its favour: an excellent road system; new trams; plenty of commercial premises; shops; schools; colleges; theatres; museums; restaurants and so on. New houses and apartments were under construction all around the region and all kinds of regeneration projects were happening in the city centre. But, in the spiritual realm, the situation was bleak.

31

Digging around

We asked two close friends, Sandra Chadwick and Christopher Summerton, both gifted intercessors and experienced in praying for cities, to begin to seek the Lord with us. Together we explored Manchester's history and prayed into some key events that had shaped it.

We were encouraged to discover, for example, that archaeologists in the 1970s discovered some of the oldest known Christian relics in Great Britain on the site of a second-century Roman fort in the Castlefield area of the city centre. They include a word square bearing the words 'Pater Noster' (Latin for 'Our Father') and date from around AD 170 . Christians came to Manchester while the ink was still wet on the first copies of the New Testament! This suggested to us that in the spiritual foundations of our city there are some godly cornerstones, despite the wholesale fallenness of subsequent generations evident in such atrocities as the Peterloo Massacre of 1819, in which hundreds of men, women and children were hacked to death by Government forces as they campaigned for political reform to empower ordinary working people. Over the years, the negative influences had gained momentum and the overall feel of our city was now distinctly evil. We prayed that God would guide us as we sought to rebuild Manchester's spiritual walls for his glory.

We sensed that in God's heart was a major spiritual regeneration plan for our city but the labourers were not yet in place. He showed us that he had all kinds of plans for new ministries in Manchester, especially to the poor and to young people. The problem was that there was such a low level of motivation, largely because of the lack of unity between Christians. If the true church across the city would only rise up, declare itself and pull together in the same direction, he could and would pour out his blessing in many different and exciting ways.

All hands on deck

In normal circumstances, building walls would be a job for skilled stonemasons. However, sometimes the task is so urgent that it's a question of all hands to the pump. Because his enemies were watching, and would attack as soon as they realised what was happening, Nehemiah recruited people from every walk of life to get the job done quickly – silversmiths, merchants, aristocracy and so on. It was vital to get the first level of defences in place as quickly as possible to provide at least a degree of protection. There would still be a lot more work to do but morale and faith would rise to new levels, and that would enable the next phase to be worked for with new confidence.

We saw things in a similar way. Our phase-one task was equally urgent. We needed to get that initial level of spiritual defence in place as quickly as possible. This was a job not just for the intercessors but for all Christians: everyone needed to get involved. If we were to strengthen our spiritual defences in the face of the enemy, we needed more than just the specialists.

We felt pretty overwhelmed by the magnitude of the task – we were just a handful of Christians with a bit of a call from God. Again, Nehemiah inspired us to remember that with God on your side even one person is a majority! In the spiritual battle between the church and the forces of darkness, prayer is one of the most powerful weapons we have at our disposal. And united, concerted prayer that binds believers together in agreement across denominational boundaries is probably the most powerful of all. If the old saying is true that 'the devil trembles when he sees the weakest Christian on their knees', then how much more terrified must he be when faced with a whole army of praying believers?!

Happy birthday

After many months of prayer, our dream had turned into a vision. Now all we needed to do was to share it with a few others and everything would be fine. At least, that's what we thought!

The first step we took was to contact a few friends from two or three other churches; these were similar to ours in style, evangelical and charismatic, non-denominational but influenced by some of the nation's recognised Christian leaders. We spoke the same language, you might say. We shared our vision with them and out of this came some initial prayer gatherings that Frank will describe in the next chapter.

Eventually, we set a date for our first public prayer event, the 23rd October 1993, a Saturday night. And, just to make sure that we would be guaranteed a decent turnout, we invited one of Britain's best-known Christian speakers, Roger Forster, co-leader with his wife, Faith, of the Ichthus Christian Fellowship in London.

We sent out thousands of flyers through established mailing lists and drove around handing out posters to dozens of churches across the city. The big day was fast approaching: Manchester's new prayer movement was about to be born.

Interestingly, I was facing another big day around the same time – one I had never expected all those months ago when this date had been set. But surely my fourth child would wait a few days until after the launch? God's sense of humour couldn't possibly extend to a double-booking of these proportions! The reason why we had originally chosen the 23rd October was because another church had been planning its own prayer meeting for that night, also to pray for the city. When they heard of our plans, they said they would happily link in with our meeting as a demonstration of a desire for unity. It was close to my due date but not so close that it seemed to matter.

However, as the day approached, my body started to send me signals that this was going to be a very close call. In fact, as you've probably guessed by now, on the Saturday morning the twinges began! By mid-afternoon, Frank and I were thanking God for the safe delivery of Matthew Adam, who weighed in at a whopping 9lbs.

Despite the physical exertion I'd gone through, I think I still half expected to be present at the prayer meeting a few hours later. In the end, common sense prevailed! Frank was left to bring the spiritual baby into the world while I drifted on a cloud of post-natal euphoria.

Off and running

As it turned out, the first ever Prayer Network gathering was a fairly inauspicious occasion. Only around sixty people turned up, although eleven different churches were represented, which encouraged us. The most remarkable factor was that many of those who came were pleasantly surprised at the numbers! People said they couldn't recall such a well-attended prayer meeting of this kind for decades! I shudder to think how different it might have been had we not had Roger as our main attraction.

At least we were off and running. God was challenging us to do the hard work of digging spiritual trenches in which to lay the foundations for the new spiritual walls. This suggested to us the need to make contact personally with the leaders of churches around the city and to share our vision with them. And so I began the practice of networking: a little-used term in those days, which actually felt a bit like knocking on doors to sell double-glazing!

Most church leaders granted me a hearing, usually a brief chat in their office over coffee. They listened politely as I shared the vision to see spiritual breakthrough in the city, and then probably forgot most of it and got back to their work. Some were too busy to take much notice – and who would blame them? We weren't anybody special; why should they listen to us? One or two were very excited about our vision and promised to present it to their church.

Our second event was another Saturday night prayer concert in March 1994. We followed the same format as before, and this time invited Gerald Coates as the star turn. Numbers rose to a staggering 80 plus and, once again, the general consensus was positive. God certainly must be up to something for people to turn out in such quantity!

I remember we prayed that night for a young evangelist called Andy Hawthorne, who gave a presentation of the ministry of The Message, which was very much in its infancy back then. God had given him a vision to present the gospel in a relevant way to teenagers in Manchester, and he was praying for open doors into more schools.

As well as delivering an inspiring message, Gerald also declared that God had given him a prophetic word for the new prayer movement. He called a few of us out to the front, and began to prophesy about how the Lord would use this new network of prayer to prepare the way for the beginnings of revival in our land. Frank and I experienced a mixture of trepidation and excitement as Gerald confidently spoke into our lives words of encouragement and promise.

We were a bit puzzled at one point when he suddenly began to repeat the number seven over and over again. 'God is giving me the figure seven for you,' he said. 'Seven, seven, seven, seven …' he must have spoken it out about 77 times! He didn't offer us any explanation or interpretation, either in the moment or later. Those who know Gerald will be familiar with his somewhat enigmatic style!

We were left pondering whether there was any significance to this number or not, and concluded that, if it was important, then God would clarify it to us some way or other. Five or six years later, as we were preparing for Soul Survivor – The Message 2000, it occurred to me that this momentous mission would be taking place seven years after the launch of the prayer movement. In the absence of anything more substantial, I'll claim that as direct fulfilment of Gerald's word, especially as Andy Hawthorne consistently makes the same connection himself.

City first

We continued to hold regular prayer gatherings and numbers increased steadily, especially once we changed to a Wednesday evening, which seemed to be a more church-friendly night than a Saturday. Some churches cancelled their own midweek prayer meeting and attended ours instead. Some even asked their home groups not to meet on those weeks, in favour of uniting with others to pray for the city.

We thought this was just like some of those in Nehemiah's day who put on hold the building of their own homes in favour of working with their neighbours to strengthen the walls of the city. There seem to be times when God asks churches to do exactly this: to prioritise, for a time, the needs of the wider area over and above their own parochial agendas.

The leaders and members of churches that did this all tell us that it was a very positive experience. They talk about the privilege it was for them to prefer the needs of the wider community. Some even say that those times were some of their most rewarding seasons of blessing for their own church. We shouldn't be surprised, though, since these are clear biblical values: as you sow, so shall you reap; seek first the kingdom of God and his righteousness and everything else will be given to you.

Soon we developed a pattern of meeting quarterly; dates were published a year in advance, which made long-term planning a lot easier for the churches. As a symbol of our unity, we organised worship bands by drawing together musicians from different churches. This involved a lot of extra work in terms of communication and rehearsals, and meant that who-ever was leading the worship had to work with a whole set of new instrumentalists and vocalists of varying degrees of ability. It was worth it, though, to know that we were living out the principles we spoke about: the reality of an inter-church worship band on display for all to see gave our evenings a strong feeling of unity right from the outset.

Step by step

Around this time, God spoke to us again. This time, it was from Deuteronomy 7:22, where he promised the occupying forces of Israel that he would drive their enemies out of Canaan in a gradual way, 'little by little'. The reason he gave to Moses was that this would prevent the ground becoming overrun by wild animals and would allow his people to possess a land that was well managed and fertile.

Frank got really excited about this, although he now refers to it as Middle-aged Man's vision, because he was weary at the time of listening to the hype of itinerant preachers who came to cities like ours with fantastic visions of what God wanted to do overnight. Phrases like 'millions swept into the kingdom' abounded at the time, along with 'the suddenlies of God' and other inspiring phrases designed to remind people of God's sovereign ability to change society at a stroke, should he so desire. The problem was that, once these prophets of glory moved on, people were left disappointed and disillusioned. Their fault, I suppose you could say, for following the illusion in the first place!

Sadly, these sensationalist approaches are still around today. Some itinerant ministries appear to need to create increasingly spectacular visions to maintain their own survival and, as fast as one generation of Christians becomes discouraged and disaffected by the lack of fulfilment of their revival prophecies, so another emerges to embrace them with relish. The New Testament warns us to beware of false prophets, and there are plenty around in every generation.

Of course, we would love to see the sort of dramatic revival that we hear being predicted from time to time, and we're certainly not denying God's ability to act so powerfully as to cause such a phenomenon. It's just that we're saddened by the way so many unaccountable, self-seeking sensationalists are allowed to distract and ultimately discourage God's people with their dramatic presentation of what they claim is the word of the Lord for today. God is not glorified when large numbers of Christians are stirred into excitement by a gifted communicator whose confident declarations turn out to be mere money-spinning mirages.

The key to interpreting any vision or word from God lies in the acknowledgement and approval it receives from a group of experienced Christians. The Bible refers to this as weighing and testing (1 Corinthians 14:29). When we considered this word, about moving forward slowly but surely, we were all convinced it was God speaking to us very specifically to encourage us to keep going even though progress may be slow. Step by step, little by little. We sensed an increase in our faith and we all agreed that this was something we could trust God for. We felt relieved that we didn't need to generate excessive enthusiasm either in advance of or indeed on the evening of our prayer gatherings.

God was building something that would last, and he was going to do it his way. We were encouraged as we saw gradual growth both in numbers and in acceptance among an increasingly broad spectrum of churches. For a while, the song, 'We want to see Jesus lifted high, a banner that flies across the land' became our theme song because its chorus is based on those words from Deuteronomy 7:22: 'Step by step we're moving forward, little by little we're taking ground, every prayer a powerful weapon, strongholds come tumbling down.'

Vision and values

By the end of 1994, after a series of small but very significant miracles (principally of the divine appointment kind that brought us into contact with key people at just the right time), we published our list of Prayer Network core group members, people who met together to plan the gatherings and who carried overall responsibility. This was not a committee but a relationally connected working group whose members loved each other, respected people's differences and celebrated a common vision and heart: to see the city transformed for Jesus through unified prayer and action.

It was great to be able to announce to the world (well, to the Christian world at least) that we had New Frontiers, Covenant

Ministries, Salt and Light and Kingdom Faith people working with Anglicans, Baptists, Pentecostals and others. In itself, this was evidence that God was clearly at work since, in those days, not only had such a grouping never been seen before but it could not even have been imagined in the minds of most believers. Our theologies and churchmanship were so varied that it would have been easier to find good reasons why we really couldn't work together.

Instead, we chose to take the disciplined and determined route of committing ourselves to working around our shared values and objectives (although we always enjoyed some stimulating discussions on our regular curry nights together!).

Here's the mission statement we put together that would serve us well for the years ahead:

VISION

Our desire is to see the spiritual atmosphere in the region of Greater Manchester transformed. We long for a move of God that will bring renewal and restoration to the church and will spill over into society at large.

In our dreams and visions we see crime rates dropping, violence decreasing, drug dealers disappearing, prostitution declining and apathy diminishing. We see business booming, housing improving, schools flourishing and hope rising. We see other cities across Europe looking at the evidence of the illuminating and seasoning effect of the kingdom of God.

We believe that such a reversal of the current situation will only come about as a result of God pouring out his Spirit upon a church united in a determined commitment to seek his face. So we aim to build a fortress of effective

41

prayer around the Greater Manchester region by helping to network together Christians from all denominations and streams.

VALUES

1. *Prayer is the key to effective change.* Spiritual warfare is much broader than just praying, but without fervent, believing prayer we can achieve very little (2 Chronicles 7:14; 2 Corinthians 10:4; Ephesians 6:10–18).

2. *Unity of purpose is possible.* We can retain our ecclesiological and theological distinctives and preferences at the same time as throwing ourselves wholeheartedly into total-agreement prayer gatherings (Psalms 133:1; Matthew 18:19–20).

3. *Relationships of honour and respect within the body of Christ must be striven for.* When we begin to demonstrate truly Christian attitudes of love towards one another we will become a powerful agency for the kingdom of God in our area (John 15:17; Galatians 5:22; Hebrews 13:1).

4. *Foundations are vital.* Our first task is to defend the region in the spiritual dimension against the rampant attacks of Satan. As Christians from different backgrounds join themselves together regularly in prayer, so the spiritual walls of the city will be gradually rebuilt (Nehemiah 2:5; Amos 9:13–15; Matthew 16:18).

5. *High-profile personalities are not necessary.* God wants to work through anonymous people. We want to see all the leaders of churches in and around Greater Manchester involved, without any taking priority or prominence (Isaiah 40:3–5; John 1:22–23).

42

6. *Progress is guaranteed.* It may well be gradual and even, at times, invisible but we walk by faith, not by sight, and take God's promises seriously. It may take many years just to build 'prayer-walls' around the city. If so, we intend to press on, step by step, until we see evidence of a real break-through in the spiritual realm (Deuteronomy 7:22).

two
radical middle ground

Frank

Working together

The latent potential of human co-operation is huge. In business, education, healthcare and government everyone these days is talking about networking, partnerships, symbiosis, synergy and teamwork as though the concept of working together for a common goal had just been discovered. In truth, people have been collaborating since the beginning of time in just about every area of life. Sayings like: 'The whole is greater than the sum of its parts' have been part of conventional wisdom for centuries.

Way back in Genesis 11 there's an amazing tale of how human co-operation was so effective in attempting to organise society in direct contradiction to the will of God that the Almighty himself was forced to intervene.

The issue was that the first humans had been commanded to fill the earth. However, instead of spreading out and multiplying all across the world, the sons of Noah were settling in one place, largely under the mutinous leadership of Nimrod the hunter (whose very name means 'let's revolt').

They were seeking to establish a way of life that would ultimately lead to the rejection of God and their own self-glorification. The Tower of Babel they were constructing was a symbol of arrogance and a monument to self-rule. The people were so unified in their objective that their success was almost inevitable.

Having promised never again to flood the earth and wipe out a generation of rebels, God this time acted in a less cataclysmic manner to steer the human race in his desired direction. The biblical account says that he decided to 'confuse their language', making it impossible for them to communicate effectively and thus stimulating the emergence of different nationalities and separate territories.

Scholars have a variety of ways of interpreting this very significant passage of Scripture. All agree, however, that the take-home point is that, left to our own devices as a race, we humans have the power to organise ourselves so efficiently that we can even defy God.

Just imagine then, how much we could serve God's purposes if we were willing and able to learn to work together in line with his plans, instead of in opposition to them! Thankfully, God's supreme intervention into our dissident human existence has made this possible. In Christ, God began the final phase of reconciling the world to himself.

The new humanity now living on the earth – the church, the body of Christ – has exactly that potential. We can co-operate together along the very guidelines of God's agenda. The outpouring of the Holy Spirit on the Day of Pentecost (Acts 2) not only signifies the birth of the newly empowered community but also symbolises the reversal of the curse of Babel. The spiritual gift of tongues enabled people of different nationalities all to hear and understand what God was saying!

Unity at the heart

One of the central themes of this book is that the principle of unity lies at the very heart of God's strategy for transforming communities throughout the world. We believe this absolutely and yet we didn't see it quite so clearly at first, even though we knew it was important. Looking back over the years, we can now see that each step we've taken along the way has been built on the need to win the broadest possible co-operation between believers of every tradition, without diluting our own strongly held evangelical/charismatic core values.

We refer to this now with a phrase we picked up about ten years ago: Radical Middle Ground. Although we'd tried for a few years to explain our position on unity, we'd always found it difficult to describe concisely how we felt called to draw together Christians from a broad spectrum of traditions to pray together for the city. One day, we were in conversation with Nick and Lois Cuthbert, from Birmingham, when they used this phrase to refer to their own stance on working with other churches. Immediately, we knew we'd stumbled across a term that summarised so much of what God was calling us to do for him: further confirmation that we were tapping into something of God's broader strategy.

For us, Radical Middle Ground describes perfectly where we position our own thinking and practice. On the one hand, ordinary middle ground is generally no man's land: a place of such compromise that any agreement reached is shallow and superficial. Too much ground has to be given away by all parties in order to find anything in common.

On the other hand, used on its own, the word radical outlaws most of those who would call themselves 'ordinary'. In some circles, it carries connotations of superiority and spiritual élitism. Used together, though, these two ideas convey the right

47

balance between deeply rooted (the actual meaning of radical) conviction and broad-minded co-operation.

Starting in our home city of Manchester, our call is to network together as many ordinary, normal, truly believing Christians as possible in prayer and harmonious kingdom action, giving ground where necessary and possible in order to build strong relationships, but standing firm in cases where the truly central doctrines of the church are not being prioritised.

What is unity?

Unity is not unanimity, where everyone must agree with everything. Nor is it uniformity, where everyone must behave in the same way. True unity is a commitment to the core values of the kingdom of God that leads naturally to co-operation. We were privileged to learn this right at the outset of our Christian lives.

Shortly after our conversions in 1980 (both within a few months of each other and in the first year of our marriage), we found ourselves taking part in a town-wide evangelistic mission. Twenty churches were working together over a one-year period, climaxing in a ten-day series of outreach meetings in the town centre. In typical new Christian fashion, we threw ourselves wholeheartedly into this and signed up for everything!

As a newly qualified English/Drama teacher, Debra found herself leading the drama group; writing and rehearsing sketches for the evening meetings. With my background in sales and marketing, I was installed as the leader of the publicity committee (there's that word again – always beware of the 'c' word!).

Every month there was a 'rally' where the evangelist Eric Delve would come and inspire the hundreds of Anglo-Metho-Bapti-Costals, all of whom would mix happily, give generously and chatter noisily long into the night while consuming vast quantities of tea from old, cracked, duck-egg blue cups.

We saw God do miracles both in the big ten-day outreach and during the mission itself. Our fundraising target was met (to the actual pound – amazingly, since the total was reached as the result of a free-will offering!); many people were converted (including many young people who are still going strong today); some were miraculously healed, and new ministries were birthed. At the heart of it all was a unity of purpose that drew people together.

During the preparation year, Debra and I had attended a different prayer meeting every night: Monday was the Methodist; Tuesday the Baptist; Wednesday the Nazarene; Thursday the C of E, and Friday the Pentecostal. Sunday was our own evening service, and one Saturday each month was the big celebration. We stayed at home on the other three Saturdays and would have had to watch TV were it not for the endless supply of testimony books!

We loved the variety and imagined, foolishly, that this sort of inter-denominational activity was business as usual for the church. Sadly, the moment the dust had settled and the working groups had been disbanded, all the unity evaporated. It was bizarre: people who only weeks before were hugging each other would barely nod in the street. We were sagely advised by one of our leaders that it wouldn't be appropriate to frequent the other prayer meetings now that the mission was over!

Thankfully, God had planted something in the two of us that refused to die: a hunger for the kind of unity between Christians that brings blessing. We hated the idea that 'they worship God in their way; we worship him in his' and were unable to break the new friendships we'd made with believers of many different 'flavours'.

49

Marching for Jesus

A few years later we found ourselves marching for Jesus: smiling at, chatting to and singing with people from other churches, without having to discover which church they belonged to! Proclaiming the name of Jesus loudly, boldly and publicly gave us enough in common to overlook whatever differences we may have had, even without knowing what they were!

No one can measure how much impact March For Jesus had around the world but we believe it was a key element in God's strategy to turn the hearts of Christians towards each other as a first step to enabling them to co-operate together in transforming their cities.

Once again, though, when March For Jesus ceased, many churches immediately reverted back to local isolationism. Like elastic bands once the pressure to stretch has been removed, they resumed their comfortable, relaxed shape once more. It was like *déjà vu* for Debra and me! But, once more, the new contacts we'd made grew into lasting relationships.

Thankfully, there are still plenty of people within most churches who have tasted the new wine of unity and will not allow their groups to drift back into self-focused stagnation. Debra is increasingly being invited to towns and cities across the UK and beyond by people who are desperate to see Christians uniting in prayer and action, and often March For Jesus is cited as a significant milestone on their own journey. Praise God for MFJ and the pioneering radicals that made it happen despite the many obstacles that stood in their way.

God's blueprint

In the very early days of what later would become Prayer Network, a group of six of us would meet once a week to seek

God together. We had a strong sense that he was calling us to some sort of inter-church activity but we had no clear idea of what it might entail.

Most of the group, with the significant exception of me, would happily refer to themselves as intercessors. Each had a clear call from God to spend a lot of time in his presence, laying before him circumstances and people that needed his intervention. They would also spend time just listening to him, searching their Bibles as they sensed his voice, and noting things down in their journals.

I have to admit that, although Debra was more comfortable than I was with the often unusual and sometimes quite bizarre behaviour of the typical intercessor, neither of us could survive any of these meetings without at least a few questions. Sometimes there would be long periods of silence; sometimes there would be wall-to-wall cacophony. Often there would be powerful words of prophecy delivered in the first-person language of an Old Testament herald, sometimes accompanied by dramatic gestures and Mount Hermon style volume!

It wasn't quite our first contact with this method of prayer but it was the first time we'd been so closely involved. If pushed, Debra and I would both have to say that all the drama seemed a bit unnecessary and sometimes quite amusing. But, at the same time, we couldn't deny that there certainly seemed to be something of God about it. So we stuck with it for months and enjoyed building relationships with one another at the same time.

One of these weekly meetings stands out in my mind. Halfway through, we were waiting on God, having spent time praising and worshipping him. Suddenly, one of our number sprang to her feet and began to pace the room.

'Show us your blueprint!' she roared at the ceiling. 'Show us your blueprint, Father!'

She repeated this so many times that I recall finding it difficult to suppress an Adrian Plass style comment! (Apologies to anyone who has never read *The Sacred Diary of Adrian Plass*: if this is you, may I suggest that you get hold of a copy as soon as you can; it's the funniest Christian book ever written.) To my credit, I resisted the temptation to air my theological reservations there and then. However, later, as we talked together, we found ourselves wrestling with the theory of whether or not God worked like that.

Did he have a spiritual blueprint for Manchester? If so, was it likely that he would reveal its details to a bunch of ordinary folk like us? What did we expect him to do – send an angel? Drop a document from the sky with step-by-step instructions on how to win the city? Write on the clouds with his finger?

These were important questions but we found ourselves unable to come up with any clear answers. We definitely believed that God had plans for our city and that we were being called to play some part in them. But we were uncomfortable with the notion that we were to be custodians of some special revelation.

We decided to walk forward cautiously and to believe that God would use us if we followed his lead, one step at a time. God probably did have a clear strategy for Manchester, we concluded, but for it to come to pass would no doubt involve many other people and lots of adjustment along the way.

God certainly is a planner: the creation bears evidence to this and Scripture teaches it. However, he also interacts with fallen people and their evolving, ever-changing circumstances in order to bring his plans to fruition. We felt that we needed to take care to be submissive and surrendered as we asked him to guide us through the initial stages. We didn't want to presume that we could present a sort of artist's impression of what God wanted to do in our city.

Looking back some twelve years later, we feel we can now see that God's blueprint was more to do with principles and values than structures or strategies. There have been many attempts in recent years to put forward detailed models for 'winning cities', and we've been influenced by most of these to a lesser or greater extent. Although there is considerable variety in all of these patterns, there does seem to be a clear common principle: the centrality of unity within the body of Christ. It's not presumptuous to say that, whatever God's specific plan may be, the idea of his people flowing together in unity is very much at the heart of it.

Unity: the key to God's strategy

The concept of Christian unity has different connotations for different people. Some hold that denominations, in and of themselves, are symbols of a divided church and barriers to unity. God is unhappy about their very existence and his ultimate plan is to do away with them all. There will be no denominations in heaven, so we ought to work towards a heaven-on-earth goal in the here and now. This view usually supports itself by pointing to the fact that non-Christians are keenly aware of the disunity of the church, which provides them with an excuse to avoid the claims of Christ on their lives.

At the other end of the spectrum of opinion there are those who believe that the denomination or stream to which they belong is the one that God favours above the rest. It may be that they actually hold theirs to be the only truly Christian church. They imagine that if God has ever approved of the others, he certainly doesn't nowadays: his hand is upon their group supremely, and they will be able to accomplish alone everything God wants to achieve. For these people, unity simply means encouraging everyone in their own constituency to agree and get on! We've met people who say they're working for unity in their city when what they really mean is unity within their own church plants in the different local areas!

In between these two extremes are various shades of opinion, including what is commonly known as ecumenism or the Ecumenical Movement. Those who belong to this camp propose toleration, and possibly even celebration of the differences between Christian groups, as long as churches and denominations can find some ways of showing the world that they are, in fact, united in some way. Each group may secretly feel that their way of being and doing is superior to the others, but they nevertheless try to reach out and connect in some way to give a visible impression of unity.

There are a number of problems with all of these views, most notably the fact that God not only seems to be tolerating the different denominations and streams but actually blessing them in different ways! It's not difficult to find examples of God's Spirit at work in every corner of the world and through every expression of the church. Wherever the gospel is proclaimed and demonstrated in compassionate action in the name of Jesus Christ, God is present and pleased.

Divine diversity

The variety of church style and structure evident in the New Testament suggests that God's plan has always been to use different approaches to reach the widest possible range of people. And the doctrinal and liturgical controversies of church history may well be viewed as healthy stages in the development of the church, since they have ultimately served to diversify God's blessing and broaden the church's impact.

We've encountered many vibrant, fruitful and faithful believers in every denomination we've come across. That includes Anglican, Baptist, Brethren, Congregational, FIEC, Lutheran, Methodist, Nazarene, New, Orthodox (Greek and Russian), Pentecostal, Roman Catholic, Salvation Army, United Reformed and many others that wouldn't fit naturally under any of these labels!

The variety of denominations reflects the range of personality styles that exists within the human race. Some people prefer to worship God in a liturgical setting, with a clear structure and form to their service. Others prefer the spontaneity of an informal gathering. Some prefer to pray quietly on their knees, using familiar words that help them connect with God and receive his grace. For others, this makes them feel awkward and God feel distant. Jumping for joy in his presence is what helps them experience him.

Imagine how impossible it would be to blend these different preferences into a meaningful service of worship! Whatever out-of-this-world experience awaits us in heaven, it will surely be a fulfilling one for everyone, not something that suits some at the expense of others. It will also be the product of God's inward work in people's lives, not some outward façade masking serious inner disagreement.

Pseudo unity

The kind of unity that pleases God must be something meaningful and substantial, not just a veneer. The church will never fool the world by dressing its windows. People will be impressed when they see the reality of the one true church, not some contrived circus of priests and pastors jumping through hoops on a platform.

I was invited to attend a so-called unity meeting some years ago in a suburban town in the north of England. Around a dozen churches had been involved in planning the event for about three months. A committee comprising one representative from each church had met, and the meeting had been carefully organised to allow an equal amount of time for the respective leaders of these churches to play a part in the proceedings. One by one these honourable figures took to the stage, each to perform a vital task.

The first, a Roman Catholic, resplendent in flowing gown and starched white collar, welcomed the congregation, explained eloquently and precisely the vision and purpose of the occasion and listed solemnly the various participating churches. As he spoke, a section of the gathering sat visibly on the edge of their pews, their faces glowing with pride.

Next, the URC minister took centre stage to introduce the first hymn. She too wore a gown, but a fairly simple one of the academic variety. She gave an excellent summary of the content of the hymn and offered some interesting insights into the life of its composer. The four ladies on the front row hung on her every word.

After the hymn, it was the Pentecostal pastor's turn. Dressed in an impressive lounge suit with a loudly patterned tie, he smiled engagingly and invited us all to pray. As his extempore prayer proceeded, his voice climbed both in pitch and volume. A group of energetic enthusiasts rose to their feet and the 'Hallelujahs' flowed as the intensity and pace of the prayer increased. As the finishing line came into view, the tempo slowed, and the dramatic pauses grew slightly longer. The more sacramental types uncurled themselves from their foetal positions just in time to murmur a grateful 'Amen' in response to the predictable: 'All God's people said ...'

Another hymn followed, this time introduced inaudibly by a rickety pensioner whose clerical collar was so large it obscured most of his face, but who was clearly the champion of two entire pews, predominantly comprising hat-wearing Baptist women.

The cabaret rolled on until the Anglican vicar mercifully beamed his dismissal prayer and the various groups removed themselves to the church hall where they huddled together tightly over their tea cups, terrified at the prospect of actually having to talk to someone from another church!

Some unity! This sort of woolly, manufactured occasion serves only to broaden the divides that exist between churches. Unity is not about occasionally tolerating one another's presence and then scurrying back to the safety of separateness; nor is it about parading our distinctives while pretending we're all the same!

Unity between Christians is about genuinely exploring the common ground of our faith and finding helpful and encouraging ways of working together under God.

At the very least, it's about happily co-existing without feeling the need to refer to the different preferences we have for style of worship or priority of doctrines. At best, unity is getting to know each other so well that we can happily put differences to one side temporarily and work together to glorify God in some sort of public way.

Biblical unity

Psalm 133 says that when God's people dwell together in unity, it is such a wonderful phenomenon that it attracts the blessing of the Lord himself.

The psalmist employs two pictures to illustrate this: one of the morning dew that appears daily on the mountains of Judah; the other of the sacred oil trickling down the head of the priest at the ceremony of anointing.

Both symbolise the presence of the Holy Spirit and the pleasure of the Father. The mountains attract God's blessing by doing nothing more than standing strong before him. The priest brings pleasure to God by bowing obediently and worshipfully in his presence.

The people of God are called simply to live together harmoniously: The Good News Bible translates this verse as 'How wonderful it is, how pleasant, for God's people to live together in harmony!' This pleases God so much that he bestows his blessing upon them. Harmony cannot happen without different notes being played together. When this is done badly, the result is discord and dissonance. However, when different notes are played well together, the effect is a beautiful blend that blesses the ear and lifts the spirit.

In what is often referred to as his high-priestly prayer, Jesus prayed that Christians everywhere might be one, as he and the Father are one (John 17:20–23), with the outcome being that the world at large would know the love of God. Unity, then, is not simply an option for us today; since Jesus has prayed for it, we can be sure that the Father is working to answer the prayer of his Son. We need to make sure that we're not actually preventing the answer to this prayer by active resistance or passive apathy.

In his letter to the church at Ephesus, Paul issues a strong command to the Christians there to 'make every effort to keep the unity of the Spirit through the bond of peace' (Ephesians 4:3). He goes on to remind his readers that there is only one church, one baptism, one faith and so on. The church at

Ephesus was made up of both Jewish and Gentile Christians, and it seems that both groups were growing apart from each other due to differences of opinion on doctrinal matters. Paul uses strong imperatives to challenge them about not only 'stopping the rot' but also reversing the trend to show the glory of God to the world.

Once again, we duck this issue at our peril. If we continue to concentrate exclusively on our own church or denomination, and not actively strive to demonstrate unity to the world, we'll find ourselves missing out on the commanded blessing of God and standing in direct contradiction to the New Testament.

The remarkable point about Paul's challenge is that it calls us not to manufacture unity but to manifest and maintain it. There is only one church, he says; our task is to make that oneness visible. We're not being asked to cobble together some sort of Ikea version of unity; we're simply being urged to express the oneness that exists within the church that Jesus is building. He's the architect and builder; we're his co-workers. He's the head, and we're the limbs. The body of Christ exists as one in the spiritual realm. But on earth that body will remain invisible unless Christians from different denominations unite and put some flesh on its bones.

Eyes wide open

Having said all that I have about unity, I nevertheless want to stress how important it is to be realistic about what we can expect in terms of Christians coming together from a diverse range of traditions across a town or city.

Many years ago, I held a far more ambitious view of what a city-wide church should look like. I dreamed of the day when all the different churches would happily rename themselves as congregations of the one Manchester church, just as it was in first-century Ephesus or Philippi (isn't it funny how no one ever uses Corinth as an example of an ideal church!).

In my dream, there was a group of city elders, appointed by the whole church to oversee city-wide events. All the separate congregations would, of course, retain their own identity, serve their own locality and conduct their own affairs according to their own traditions and values. But there would always be clear agreement about 'city church' matters and everyone would be happy.

Nowadays, however, I have come to realise that this utopian model is neither realistic nor in God's plan. Even so, I regularly find myself listening to someone (usually at least ten years younger) outlining the same dream and challenging me to 'lay down my own local ministry' in favour of such an ideal!

Realistic unity is about releasing one another into the freedom of our different theological emphases, styles of worship and so on. It's about enjoying our diversity while at the same time agreeing on our core Christian beliefs and values. It's about cultivating attitudes of humility and respect, preferring each other in love and speaking well of one another (which is much more than just not speaking negatively about each other; and even this can be a challenge sometimes).

Realistic unity is nothing at all to do with structures and committees, steering groups and boards of trustees, formal constitutions and legal agreements. It's about relationships of love and trust that allow God's creative Spirit to flow like a river into the desert places of our land in his way and in his timeframe. If we can learn to aim for the ideal in our principles but settle for the real in practice we'll find a unity that is achievable, valuable and beautiful.

three
gathering leaders

Debra

Respect for the role

Hindsight always provides higher ground, and as we reflect on what God has done in Manchester we need to be careful not to give the impression that we knew exactly what we were doing. Although we had a clear sense of calling and a sharp vision of prayerful, cross-church unity that would defend the city in the spiritual realm and pave the way for new expressions of the kingdom of God, we had no advance list of objectives. We simply sensed the latest nudge from the Holy Spirit and tried our best to obey it. This is especially true when we consider how God led us to draw together leaders of churches, an activity of which even the mention can cause eyebrows to be raised in some circles.

We knew instinctively right from the start of Prayer Network that we ought at least to keep leaders informed of what we were organising. As local church leaders ourselves, Frank and I often felt uncomfortable about many events that were organised to which Christians from any and every church were invited without any contact being made with their pastors/overseers/

ministers. Even if only out of respect for their role, it was right for them to be notified of gatherings that may attract their members.

We believe that the church is the primary agent of God's kingdom and that he appoints leaders to a place of high responsibility. Much is expected of local church leaders: not only are they to serve 'the flock' diligently by enabling pastoral care and public worship, teaching and preaching, evangelism, administration and so on, but also they are accountable to God for all of this. It's really important, therefore, that anyone attempting to gather Christians across a town or city does so with the maximum co-operation of the respective local leaders.

We always encouraged those attending our meetings to talk to their leaders and to pass on to them our literature outlining the aims and values of Prayer Network. We even suggested that, in some cases, it may be necessary for people to ask their leaders for permission to be involved, since that's the way some churches view the leader/member relationship.

Looking back, however, we can see that there is much more to it than mere politeness. Leaders of the church of Jesus Christ carry significant responsibility for the spiritual climate of a city. As agenda-setters, they shape attitudes and organise activities that either maintain parochialism and fragmentation or move in the direction of co-operation and unity.

Even at the purely practical level, leaders act as the communication hub of their church or organisation. Mail usually crosses their desk and often stays there for a long time before being filed away (often in the bin!) or redirected to someone else to be dealt with.

Busy as most pastors and ministers are, they can't and shouldn't be bypassed, even with the best intentions. I found out quite quickly that the most effective way of gaining the support and participation of a local church was to contact the key leader by phone and make an appointment to visit them. Once there, I would outline the vision and ask them to nominate someone else to be the contact person in the future. In most cases, these initial personal contacts developed into long-term links with the key leader themselves. These connections developed into a relational network through years of regular contact that allowed trust and confidence to develop. All this was to prove vital when it came to organising city-wide missions such as Soul Survivor/Message 2000 and Festival Manchester, which we'll talk about in more detail later.

In the city gates

At the spiritual level, there is a sense in which leaders act as the gatekeepers of the town or city, and they don't need to be conscious of this for it to be true. God has appointed people in roles of responsibility and authority and he expects them to represent him and enable his people to follow his direction in advancing his kingdom.

In our case, the reconstruction of spiritual city walls was clearly a priority from God's perspective and, looking back, we can see how he led us across the paths of many different leaders, constantly giving us favour as we sought to establish new relationships from scratch. We're sure, now, that without the participation of so many figures of spiritual responsibility in the city, our vision for inter-church prayer would never have got off the ground at all.

Once again, the experience of Nehemiah and his call to rebuild the broken walls of ancient Jerusalem relates closely to what was happening to us in Manchester. Of particular interest to me, as I studied the story closely, was the way that the spiritual leaders were the first to start the building work and that this, in turn, seemed to have inspired people from all walks of life to follow their example.

In Chapter 3 of Nehemiah, it's Eliashib the high priest who makes the first move. He is followed by the other priests, and then by a long list of different people, from perfume-makers and goldsmiths to rulers of districts! And it wasn't just the big strong men that went to work; a number of women are also mentioned, including the daughters of Shallum – suggesting either that these were unusually strong ladies or that the urgency of the task was such that just about every able-bodied person got involved.

It's also interesting that Eliashib started the rebuilding project by concentrating on the Sheep Gate. All the access points to the city had been burnt by invaders and needed to be restored in order to make the new walls secure. The Sheep Gate was the one nearest the Temple, through which animals were brought to be sacrificed. The fact that the high priest chose to begin the whole project by repairing this gate and dedicating it again to the Lord underlines both the importance of prayer and the necessity for spiritual leaders to act as role models.

Unity in a city or town begins with the house of God and specifically with leaders. Those entrusted with spiritual leadership are called to be a model and example to all the other groups across the city. Leaders carry a responsibility to begin and to maintain the work of unity and transformation.

Chickens or hedgehogs?

I don't want to give the impression that networking with church leaders is easy. I remember frequently feeling a little intimidated at the prospect of phoning new people, particularly those from streams or denominations that I was not familiar with. Moreover, as a woman, I knew I may not always be taken seriously as a leader. Amazingly, however, doors opened easily and the vast majority of my 'cold calls' were very positive experiences at a personal level. God was clearly at work, and I was very grateful that he seemed to be granting me favour. More and more churches came on board as leaders gave their blessing, and our regular prayer events grew in attendance and profile as a result.

The next stage, though, was more daunting. The call to unity was clearly coming not only to the church at large but also to its shepherds. In one of our prayer times as a core group, God spoke to us through Matthew 23:37, where Jesus laments over Jerusalem's reluctance to be unified under his 'wings'. He showed us that it was his desire not only to gather the members of his church together for prayer and action but also to draw their leaders together.

We were pleased to see a growing number of leaders attending our regular prayer gatherings, and we usually involved them during the evening by asking them either to come forward to lead a prayer slot or to allow people to gather around them in their seats and pray for them. However, we noticed that they tended to stay with their own groups of people and didn't seem to mix easily with their counterparts from other churches.

In Matthew 23:37, Jesus was saying that he wanted to gather his leaders together like a mother hen gathers her young. However, the leaders' body language made them seem more like hedgehogs than chicks! They appeared to be acutely aware of even the tiniest matter of belief or practice that may not be shared by another group and typically adopted a protective approach to their own territory and 'flock'.

Generally speaking, we found that ordinary Christians warmed quite readily to the prospect of mixing together at large events; in fact, many are involved in work-based unity groups already: Christian unions, or societies like Christians in Caring Professions; Christian Police Association; Christian Medical Fellowship; Christian Teachers' Association and so on, all of which draw their members from across the denominational spectrum. Ordinary believers, it seems, have always been keen to remove barriers and express their oneness in Christ. They instinctively seem to appreciate one another as co-members of his body and, generally speaking, don't seem too bothered by the doctrinal differences that are supposed to keep them at arm's length from each other. Their leaders, however, tend not to share this natural propensity to relax in each other's company.

Suspicious minds

As Frank and I got to know more and more leaders in Manchester, it became clear that one of the main reasons for the lack of unity between them was suspicion. There had been a considerable amount of 'recycling of saints' in our city during the past decade or so, just as there had in many other areas of the UK.

New waves of renewal, restoration or revival (depending on your preference) had swept the church, bringing new emphases on different aspects of the Christian life. High-profile Christian leaders who had established new churches on the back of big-budget conferences and postmodern pew-fillers were voting with their feet on the basis of current market appeal. As a result, many church leaders seemed reluctant even to talk to each other, let alone develop any sort of friendship. We were saddened, but not surprised, by how difficult it was to encourage leaders to consider that God might be calling them to relate together more closely.

66

Here's an example of the sort of thing that was happening. A young man in our church asked if he could have a word with Frank after a Sunday morning service. He produced a word-processed letter from a well-known church that had established itself in the city centre a few years ago and that regularly hosted conferences featuring internationally known speakers. The letter was not only personally addressed to this guy, who had been a committed member of our church for many years, but also included his name in three or four places in the body of the text. 'Dear Dave,' it read, 'It was great to meet you recently at the conference. We trust the Lord ministered to you and blessed you.' No problem so far, but when the letter went on to explain that Dave had been added to the rota for serving refreshments at their regular Sunday service the following week the whole thing took on a different light! He was upset that this church had assumed by his attendance at a conference that he was interested in joining them (and, therefore, leaving us) and we were dismayed that such overt poaching should be happening in the guise of equipping the body of Christ.

The more we talked to leaders, the more convinced we became that God wanted to soften their hearts towards each other and to realise that his plans for the city were more important than their own insecurities. That he wanted to gather them together in a place of comfort, warmth and protection. We prayed for guidance as to how we might begin to work towards a solution. Already we'd seen God break down many barriers that had previously appeared impregnable; our core group relationships were a good example of this: perhaps the same sense of trust and friendship that we were enjoying could overflow to a wider group of leaders in the city.

Leadership loneliness

Another common factor we came across among ministers and pastors was that many seemed to be quite lonely. Some, of course, were happily working as part of a team with lots of support from their colleagues and, in many cases, from other leaders within their denomination or stream (although, even in these cases, there were many who suffer the 'lonely in a crowd' syndrome because they couldn't really be themselves in these circles).

We often found ourselves listening to stories of unhappy isolation: leaders who felt that no one understood the specific pressures they faced and who didn't dare share their feelings with anyone in their church for fear of being misunderstood. Many were frustrated about their workload and what they felt were unrealistic expectations of their congregation.

Some had financial problems; some were struggling with intellectual challenges to their faith; some were feeling like they were under constant spiritual attack; some were so discouraged that they felt like giving up the ministry altogether.

Aside from the personal issues, the majority of leaders we spoke to said that they didn't feel like they were playing any part in the city other than the contribution they were making in their immediate area. They often didn't know about some events until it was too late to plan them into their church calendar or, by contrast, sometimes got invited to attend two things on the same date.

As we continued to pray, God spoke to us about creating a safe haven for leaders across the city. A regular opportunity to meet together for fellowship, for prayer, for mutual encouragement and to keep in touch with events and activities that were being organised in and around Manchester. Naturally, this would be a useful way of reminding everyone of our quarterly prayer gatherings but we also wanted to make leaders aware of conferences, concerts, missions, seminars and so on; in this way, we hoped to reach a wider group with the relevant publicity and prevent date clashes over the forthcoming months.

Let's do lunch

We shared our vision with one or two others and were encouraged by their response. We felt that a regular lunch slot would be the most accessible for busy leaders and that somewhere close to the city centre would work best. So, in 1997 we launched the Prayer Network Leaders' Lunch programme.

We would meet weekly, on a Friday, in a neutral venue near the university. It was a building owned by the Methodist Church, with a meeting-room that would seat about 100 people. We had to pay a nominal amount to use the hall and kitchen, and the deal included a couple of beaming women who served tea and biscuits with a welcome and winsome Caribbean enthusiasm. Lunch would be of the 'bring-your-own' variety: it wasn't the food that mattered but the fellowship.

On the first Friday there were four of us: Frank, me, Michael Harvey, a businessman who had been a strong supporter of Prayer Network from its inception and a member of the core group, and Eric Berrisford, who describes himself as God's washer-up, not a leader in any sense but a man with a huge heart for unity and a calling to serve in the background in a variety of practical ways.

It was hardly a dynamic group of key movers and shakers! Over the next few weeks our numbers fluctuated between four and five as we were joined a couple of times by Colin Barron, the senior leader of the Manchester Family Churches. Colin encouraged us that we were on the right track, saying that he really believed it was God's heart to gather leaders regularly in a city like ours. He also felt that Frank and I were anointed for this and promised to support us in our attempt to carry out God's call. This was a timely boost, as we were both wondering whether we were barking up the wrong tree since, despite our best efforts, we were failing to attract any new people at all.

We analysed and prayed about what we were doing and why it hadn't taken off in the way we'd imagined it would, and came to the conclusion that both the venue and the frequency were wrong. Our reason for choosing a neutral place to meet was based on the idea that leaders would be uncomfortable going to 'someone else's place'. We didn't want to give the impression that any particular church was setting itself up over others, especially given the existing sense of competition between some. And the idea of meeting weekly was supposed to enable relationships to grow quickly as leaders met repeatedly, even allowing for absences each time.

Colin urged us to host the lunch meetings at our own building and not to care what one or two might think of our motives. God would judge, he reminded us, and if he was anointing us then we shouldn't fall prey to false modesty. We deferred to his guidance and also decided to sacrifice our idealistic weekly programme for a realistic monthly one. We switched to a Wednesday and replaced the 'BYO' model with a lunch-provided one.

Trolley dash

On the morning of the first new-style Leaders' Lunch, Frank and I scrambled around Tesco's loading a trolley with baguettes, cheese, milk and chocolate biscuits, with absolutely no idea of how many to cater for. We decided to err on the side of excess rather than risk embarrassment by serving our guests with too little, and spent the next two hours buttering bread and setting out chairs.

An encouraging turnout of around 30 people made short work of every last crumb, and we were exhausted by the time we'd cleared up and put the chairs away.

We'd spent half an hour or so just mingling and eating, saying hello to each other and making small talk while a Graham Kendrick tape played in the background. After inviting everyone to sit down, we switched off the music and asked each person in turn to introduce themselves to the group, say which church or ministry they represented and tell us a little about themselves.

Once everyone had done that, we asked them to split into groups of three, share a prayer request each and pray for one another. That was it. An hour and a half had flown by and we finished, as we'd promised we would, at two o' clock.

We asked people to log their contact details as they left and to bring a colleague or a ministry friend to the next lunch in a month's time. Frank then disappeared into the kitchen to help Eric with his pot-washing ministry while I carried on chatting to those who were in no hurry to leave.

It had been a really uplifting time. As well as renewing contact with 20 or so leaders we already knew, we also met a number of new people, some of whom had not been in Manchester for long and had, that day, made their first contact with other leaders with similar values. Apparently, many of the more localised 'fraternals' were formal and strained. Our goal of providing a safe haven seemed to be a big step closer already.

Divisions disappear

Over the next few months we saw numbers rise steadily as more leaders came along from the city and its surrounding suburbs. On average, there would be around 70 or 80, rising to over 100 on occasions.

By now, we had a team of keen volunteer lunch-makers led by our friend, Joy Wright, who has a clear spiritual gift of hospitality. What a relief for Frank and me, neither of whom has even a hint of that anointing! We could now concentrate on welcoming people and facilitating introductions while everyone feasted on a range of open sandwiches, chicken legs, pizza slices and so on. The days of bread and cheese were fading fast into history!

We stuck with the tight format of half an hour of mingling and munching followed by an hour of interviews, prayer and updates on imminent events. Occasionally, we invited a speaker from another city or a national ministry to come and inspire us. We always finished at two o' clock sharp, allowing those who needed to leave to do so without any awkwardness, although the majority would linger, chat and finish off the remains of the buffet.

The feedback we received ranged from simple appreciation to glowing praise as people enjoyed each other's company and felt a sense of belonging to something wider than their every-day corner of the vineyard.

One young Pentecostal minister confided to us on one occasion that these lunch meetings were his lifeline at a time when he was struggling so much in a church that seemed to be resisting everything he did. A single man, there was no one he could unburden himself to apart from his brothers and sisters at the Leaders' Lunch. 'They don't judge me,' he explained, 'and because they experience similar challenges they understand exactly what I'm going through.' He knew they wouldn't break his confidence and he appreciated their prayers. Many others have said similar things over the years and it's a great source of encouragement to us that God has used this group to bring healing and hope at a personal level.

Barriers rapidly lowered and even disappeared completely as leaders got to know each other as ordinary human beings and colleagues in the wider church. Appreciation for one another grew as common values were recognised and a sense of agreement emerged on behalf of the city. New friendships began and led to new practises, like preaching in each others' churches (thus risking the exposure of one's flock to dangerous doctrinal impurities!), loaning of a PA and other equipment, using another church's baptistry and so on.

One major development greatly furthered the wider cause when a large church that owns a converted city-centre ware-house agreed to make its building available for inter-church gatherings, and to do so at no cost. As the building became increasingly used by different groups, even more perceptions of difference and division were overcome to the point at which they ceased to matter at all to most people. One leader told us: 'As a youngster, I was taught by my leaders that this church was not interested in working with others and never would be. What a privilege it is to be able to be a part of something that's moving away from such unhelpful prejudices.'

Trust and respect grew steadily between leaders across the city, paving the way for exciting co-operative outreach ventures from On the Move, which involved dozens of churches in barbecue evangelism all around the city, to Festival Manches-ter, which involved 500 active partner churches (more about this in Chapter 10).

Nowadays, there is a growing move towards a number of Manchester churches regularly organising their Alpha weekends together. On the practical level, it's a mystery that this hasn't happened before now: the pooling of transport, accommodation, administration and ministry resources means greater efficiency and lower stress levels for everyone. And the larger numbers mean a very exciting group dynamic that seems to allow the Holy Spirit to move more powerfully. In reality, though, the concept of church leaders sharing their potential new converts with other churches even for a weekend would have been unthinkable ten years ago. Praise God for the amazing change we're seeing in the way leaders are relating to each other nowadays.

All welcome!

One thing we always tried to do at the Leaders' Lunches was to welcome to the city any new ministries that were moving in. When there was a new church being planted we'd invite the leaders and pray for them. There is plenty of room in a city like ours for more churches, despite the perceived threat that some of us feel when a new one is launched. While over 90 per cent of our population are in the 'hatch, match and dispatch' camp of church attendance we need all the help we can get to reach them with the good news.

Pastor Matt Beemer, the senior leader of World Harvest Bible Church, often speaks of the pleasant surprise it was to be welcomed and prayed for by the leaders of existing churches when he and his wife Julie moved to Manchester to plant their church from scratch in 1997. Matt reflected: 'We knew no one and were desperate to make contact with some other churches in the city but we were afraid that our arrival might be misunderstood. As missionaries from the USA, we were quite accustomed to being viewed as something less than a blessing by British Christians, I think there was a feeling that Americans didn't always respect the British way of doing things.'

In the early days of their arrival, they heard about our lunch meetings and turned up to one on their own in fear and trepidation, only to be blown away by the warmth and support they received. They shared their vision to establish a missionary-sending church complete with Bible school and outreach facilities in the heart of one of the city's poorest areas. We prayed for their success and prosperity, asking the Lord to grant them the desires of their heart, which were mainly to do with reaching the disillusioned and disempowered.

They now have their own building, which is filled to capacity for two Sunday services and includes a day nursery and a café. Their Bible school was launched in 2004 and has 25 full-time students. Matt is adamant that they couldn't have achieved so much so quickly without the support and encouragement of other leaders in the city.

Iron sharpening iron

I don't want to give the impression that church leaders in our city have surrendered their distinctives in the pursuit of unity. People still belong to their streams and denominations with as much commitment and enthusiasm as ever. The big difference is that we are all increasingly relaxed about agreeing to differ on what are secondary issues of faith and practice.

In fact, for me, one of the highlights of being involved with leaders from a variety of backgrounds is the way that each perspective is able to inform and even gently influence the other. It's one aspect of my work that I enjoy most of all, not only because I learn so much from other leaders but also because I love to see God work so amazingly through the diversity of agendas and views. I have sat in planning meetings where almost every possible theological angle on an issue has been aired and, instead of feeling uncomfortable, everyone seemed at ease and, in the end, God's will prevailed.

Recently, I was chairing a meeting to explore ways of building on some of the partnerships we've birthed in recent years between churches, police and local authorities (more about this in Chapter 10). Those present included a quiet, yet focused young woman who works for a charity that campaigns for social justice, an outspoken evangelist, a newly converted, hard-nosed businessman, an Anglican bishop and a couple of senior leaders from free churches that stand at almost opposite ends of the ecclesiological spectrum.

We only had an hour or so to try to agree on what might be the focus of a new prayer strategy that would build on the answers to prayer we've seen in recent years in terms of crime reduction. At one point, the variety of opinions and suggestions was so great that a neutral observer might have wondered if we had anything in common at all! By the end of our time together, though, we managed to agree a mission statement that reflected something of each person's contribution and yet retained a sharp and clear focus that would keep us all moving in the same direction: Enabling partnerships between churches, police and local authorities to pray for a sustained reduction in crime and to work together to confront its causes.

We had to allow all kinds of comments to remain unaddressed and a number of questions to stay unanswered but such was our sense of common purpose that this just didn't matter. I can honestly say that working with leaders from different traditions is one of the most enriching aspects of my work these days and I thoroughly commend it. We all learn so much about our shared Christian tradition when we allow ourselves to be exposed to its many different expressions.

four
pillars of society

Frank

What to pray for

When it comes to organising large-scale, regular prayer gatherings, one challenge is to steer and direct the prayer times in a way that is meaningful and avoids controversial issues unless you believe strongly that the Holy Spirit wants this.

One has to remember that, given the broad spectrum of churchmanship in attendance, what seems to be a fairly obvious matter for prayer to one person may not even translate into the language of another. We found that each time we gathered there would inevitably be a number of different agendas represented, and it was an impossible task to include them all and keep everyone happy.

One night, for example, a very well spoken, smartly dressed, middle-aged man came to the front during a worship time and said that God was showing him a picture of the spiritual realm above Manchester: he could 'see' a complex labyrinth of interconnecting spiritual powers, each bearing different names, like Greed, Pride, Football and so on. The biggest and most powerful of these principalities, he explained, was called Homosexuality, and it was this spiritual stronghold above all others that needed to be overthrown. Debra thanked him and promised that we would weigh and test his contribution.

Seconds later, another eager participant appeared. She was a petite thirty-something who was clearly quite stirred up about something. 'Marriage,' she stated baldly, staring intensely into our faces. 'That's what we need to pray about.' And she proceeded to rattle off statistics about how divorce was increasing in our society, insisting that we ought to devote the rest of the evening to praying for Christian marriage. A friend of hers, who used to be a satanist, had told her that devil-worshippers the world over were 'praying' against Christian marriages, seeing them as strategic targets in the battle.

Although we didn't disagree that both these subjects were important and that Christians certainly should be praying about them, our sense was that neither ought to be allowed to dominate a Prayer Network evening.

The homosexuality issue is huge in Manchester: one particular section of the city centre contains so many bars and restaurants catering exclusively for homosexuals that it's known as the Gay Village, and Manchester is apparently vying with Amsterdam for the title Gay Capital of Europe. Our city council seems proud of the fact that there is a thriving gay community in Manchester and does all it can to promote its existence and champion the cause of homosexual rights. Naturally, this causes offence to many, especially the majority of Christians, some of whom feel very strongly indeed about the issue.

But the subject is not as simple as some suggest. Within the church at large there are many shades of opinion about homosexuality. Most Christians (though certainly not all) agree that the practice of homosexual sex is wrong. Most (though certainly not all) would accept that homosexual orientation is not the same as moral error, and many would accept that celibate, same-sex intimacy is OK. Clearly, it would be unhelpful to raise an issue as controversial as this in the context of a large, inter-church prayer meeting, without a good deal of forethought.

Marriage, while not in the same league in terms of face-reddening or vein-popping potential, is a subject equally fraught. Single Christians are understandably fed up of being made to feel like second-class members of the body of Christ. It seems to them that marriage, along with child-rearing and suburban-semi-owning, is a minimum standard for discipleship in our society. When the Christian marriage enthusiasts climb onto their hobby-horses and begin extolling its virtues and bemoaning its current vulnerability, singles not only feel excluded but also patronised and hurt.

Those whose marriages are less than perfect feel equally uncomfortable at times like this. The shiny idealism that tends to characterise the Christian marriage image seems so far removed from the average couple's struggle with day-to-day reality. Not to mention single parents, whose self-esteem is constantly bumping along the bottom, or remarried divorcees, who never really know if they are unconditionally accepted in church.

Focused prayer

Between meetings, we would also hear from people who felt strongly about many specific topics and they would urge us to feature them for prayer on future occasions. Israel was a big one: the potential for Christian disagreement on the Holy Land is huge! The European Union, global warming, the social problems in East Timor and so on – the list seemed endless and, we had to admit, mostly unrelated to Manchester.

The concept of theming our evenings began to crystallise in our thoughts, and it wasn't long before we had a strong sense that we'd stumbled upon another element of God's unfolding plans. We would set the meetings up well in advance to focus on an issue that was at the core of the life of the city, something that was on the hearts and minds of people in general, and where Christians were playing specific roles.

We thought about the core elements of society, aspects of everyday life that mattered to everyone and that God wanted to see renewed and restored by the salt and light of his church. We set aside an evening for the core group to pray, and within the first 20 minutes we were unanimous that our next meeting would focus on children and young people, a theme we were to revisit many times over the next few years.

With nearly three months to plan, we had plenty of time to research the subject and to contact the many different groups that were working with kids all over Manchester, some Christian, others not. Our aim was to put together a handout for the evening that would give some basic information about the numbers, needs, opportunities and challenges facing the children of Manchester and the teachers, youth workers and others who cared for them and worked with them.

We would also list the various different agencies and give prayer points and contact details so that people who came to the event would have something really useful to take away with them as a prayer resource.

Engage brain

This kind of intelligent praying became one of our strong distinctives as the movement grew. Not everyone liked it but we never felt it was necessary or possible to please everyone. It gave us substantial facts on which to base our thinking and specific needs to bring to God. It also honoured the people whose work we were hearing about and helped create new networks of support and prayer for them.

The feedback we continue to get tells us that this approach to prayer is very much appreciated, not only by wrinklies like us members but also by young people, many of whom are surprisingly comfortable in well-organised meetings with thought-through content.

We frequently change our plans during the evening to accommodate prophetic contributions or simply to wait on God in response to something that has been shared. We also vary the style and structure of the prayer slots to maintain pace and interest. However, we do so from a programme that has been prayerfully and logically put together and is based on carefully gathered research and specific prayer requests. Our Radical Middle Ground approach still seems to optimise the participation of the widest possible spectrum of churchmanship, age and social background.

Kids' stuff

We decided that, since the focus for the first of our new-look evenings was to be children, we would hold the meeting in a school. We challenged suburban Christians to venture into uncharted waters and come and pray in an inner-city school.

The turnout was encouraging – around 300 – and this included a lot of new people, drawn specifically by the theme and/or by their local links with the place we were using. We found out from subsequent feedback that many more would have attended had the venue not been off the beaten track.

Since then, we have always tried to use buildings that are well known or at least easy to locate, and we always publish a small map on the publicity flyer.

The evening was a real success. There were dozens of teachers present (including three or four heads), school governors, classroom assistants, nursery nurses, playgroup leaders and volunteer helpers from all kinds of organisations.

Many of these were not Christians but they appreciated our concern and were more than happy for us to pray for them. This would become a key characteristic of all our subsequent gatherings: inviting people who may not be Christians to come and be affirmed and appreciated as well as being prayed for. We've stopped being surprised now at how keen such people are to take part in what we previously imagined would be off-putting for them. The secret, we've discovered, is simply to assume they are believers and talk to them using the same language you would use with your Christian friends. This inclusive approach builds bridges and sends signals of trust and support, often paving the way for the Holy Spirit to work in the person's life at a deep and unguarded level.

Among the many different Christian groups in attendance that evening was Aslan, a children's dance and drama outreach group that specialised in open-air performances in shopping centres. They presented one of their pieces based on the triumph of Good over Evil accompanied by a backing track from a pop song. A Christian puppet ministry entertained us with some excellent biblical fun and the city-centre Christian bookshop put on a display of children's Bibles, tapes, videos and resources for every age.

There were children's workers from a range of churches who seemed amazed that they were being recognised and appreciated in such a big way. One young man was near to tears at the end as he shared with the gathering how invisible he felt in his church as a volunteer kids' worker. His leaders kept on challenging him to make himself available to be trained as a home group leader, a role deemed to be of greater significance for some reason. He said that God had that night confirmed to him the importance of his call to work with children, a comment that was echoed by many others.

One great feature of evenings like these is that we often hear of very practical, and sometimes very swift, answers to prayer. At the end of this particular night, a young man approached us beaming from ear to ear. He was the administrator of the Pais Project, a youth outreach ministry that we had prayed for earlier. One of the specific points they had raised was their urgent need of a computer for their office. Apparently, within minutes, they had been promised one by someone sitting in the row behind!

Healthcare

Over the following years, our themes continued to focus on what we refer to as the pillars of society: main spheres of work and service that together provide much of the infrastructure of everyday life. We prayed, for example, for those involved in the world of healthcare and chose a well-known venue situated close to one of the city's largest hospitals.

The place was packed to the doors with clinicians, dentists, ambulance crews, physiotherapists, nursing auxiliaries, hospital porters, surgeons, administrators, nurses, consultants, GPs and medics of all kinds. All of these added to the hundreds of ordinary Christians who wanted to show their appreciation by praying for the people who serve in these roles, many of whom are not just working in healthcare but are conscious of God's specific calling to their particular role.

Again, we interviewed Christians and non-Christians alike, asking them about their work and the special challenges they face. The number of excessive hours being put in by junior doctors was difficult for us to believe. One young man had had only two days off in the last month; he had worked non-stop for the last three days and nights, snatching catnaps in the rest room when possible, and was having trouble stringing a sentence together. We prayed briefly for him then sent him home to sleep!

A nurse told us how much she earned in her full-time shift-work role. She explained how, after paying her rent and living costs the week before, she hadn't had enough left to buy a birthday present for her mother. Of course, we're all aware of the existence of these kinds of facts but seeing the evidence in real life has a powerful impact. Our prayers were offered with a greater sense of conviction and even a degree of anger at the injustices suffered by so many who give so much.

One of the Christian ministries we prayed for that evening was a newly established group known as Barnabus (not a common spelling mistake this time: Barnabus is actually a double-decker bus, but not one that carries passengers; Peter and Beryl Green use the bus to take medical care to homeless people in city-centre Manchester. It's been converted to include a mobile doctor's surgery with a reception/chatting area and consulting room downstairs, and a clinic room, toilet and prayer room upstairs).

In spite of the city council's formal insistence that there are no homeless people in Manchester, the Barnabus team comes across dozens every night, many of whom are in desperate need of basic healthcare. Most of us didn't know until that night that GP and dental care are only available on the NHS to people with a fixed address. A homeless person is entitled to emergency treatment in a hospital casualty ward but can't get a rotten tooth removed by a local dentist or antibiotics for a throat infection from a GP.

Peter and Beryl explained all this and asked for prayer for all kinds of specific equipment and medical supplies, as well as more volunteer medical staff. They were inundated with enquiries at the end, and they refer back to that evening as a turning-point in their ministry. We were so impressed with Barnabus that we 'adopted' them, featuring them for prayer as often as we could. Their work has grown significantly over these last ten years and, despite very many challenges and setbacks, they continue to have a powerful impact at street level to Manchester's hungry and hurting homeless.

Equality

In 1996, we sensed God speaking to us about a number of aspects around the whole idea of oneness. Our city, like so many others, was fractured and fragmented socially, economically and geographically. Unity was not merely an issue for the church; it was also fundamental to God's desire for cities. People ought to live in harmony together, regardless of their many differences, and yet discord seemed to characterise life in twentieth-century Manchester.

Galatians 3:28 was at the core of what we believed to be a call to pray for equality between people-groups across the city: 'There is neither Jew nor Greek, slave nor free, male nor female, for you are all one in Christ Jesus.' We became more aware than ever of the deep divisions between the many different ethnic groups in Manchester. Racism was as evident as it had ever been, in spite of decades of government attention.

The huge differences in lifestyle between people living in the suburbs and those in the inner city was another issue, as were the continuing tensions between women and men and young and old. God was calling Christians to acknowledge this, and to pray urgently for healing. More than this, though, also to model to the world the genuine oneness that exists between believers regardless of age, sex, colour or wealth.

The first subject we tackled was that of equality between races. Hundreds of black, white, brown and yellow Christians packed into the Methodist Central Hall in the city centre for an evening of joyful celebration of our equality in Christ. Added into the mix was confession, repentance and a declaration of intent to work harder than ever at demonstrating the truth of our oneness in God in practical ways.

It was a rare and precious evening filled with goodwill, hope and a genuine sense of family. There were moments of great poignancy as representatives of different races spoke personally of their own experience of rejection and the subsequent lowering of their self-esteem. One black leader spoke of the subtle ways in which he'd felt excluded as a young boy even within Christian circles. He told how he'd been made to doubt whether he was even a child of God in the same sense as the white kids. Perhaps, he'd concluded, he was really one of God's stepchildren.

And there were moments of elation as we all expressed our common membership of Christ's church by spreading around the room and embracing as many different skin colours as possible within a two-minute slot and then by linking arms around the auditorium to sing together a song written specially for the occasion. Andy Britton, a friend of ours from King's Way Independent Methodist Church, had composed 'We will break dividing walls', which powerfully declared our determination to show the world how to live in one accord. Tears of joy ran freely throughout the night, even down the faces of some of the staunchest of the stiff-upper-lipped brigade.

Over the next three meetings, we followed a similar approach in addressing the urban/suburban divide, sexism and ageism – gathering large numbers of representatives from both sides of each issue, researching and communicating facts and figures that showed the true extent of the problem, expressing love, acceptance and respect from one group to the other, and promising in prayer to become part of God's solution from that point onwards.

These were powerful occasions where the Holy Spirit moved in power not only upon the gathering as a whole but also in individual hearts and minds. We've had countless messages reporting back on how challenged and changed many were as a result of these prayer times.

It would, of course, be nonsense to claim any kind of conclusive victory after one evening of prayer but we did, at least, do something to address the different expressions of inequality of which we were aware.

We named and shamed an important social issue and placed ourselves at the disposal of Almighty God, who alone can complete the task of redeeming our fallenness. 'Step by step, we're moving forward, little by little we're taking ground, every prayer a powerful weapon ...'

We often remind people that prayer is a powerful first step but it's only a first step. Having taken it, we need to repeat it again and again, relying on the Holy Spirit to fill us with the love and power of God so that we can move towards the point where, one day, we will see strongholds not only weakening but tumbling down.

There can't be any place in the church for the social inequalities that are so prevalent in our world. The community of believers needs to model radical love and acceptance across all such boundaries in a highly visible way, so that the outside world will see and know the reality of God's love in action.

Government

Praying for those in authority is one of the church's responsibilities (1 Timothy 2:1–2) and so it wasn't difficult for us to agree on this as a theme for one of our evenings. We invited local councillors and MPs, and surprised them as they took to the stage by thanking them publicly for serving with diligence and enthusiasm. We told them that their hard work was appreciated not only by us and others in their constituencies but also by the Lord himself.

Aside from our personal views or political persuasions, we all recognised that each of our guests that evening deserved the loud and sustained round of applause that happened spontaneously as Debra finished her introductions and opening comments. One by one, they recounted similar tales of long hours and demanding workloads. A common thread was the lack of appreciation each person felt, although none was complaining, simply accepting that this was par for the course.

There were tears in the eyes of most of them as they received our words of gratitude and praise. One former MP told us later that this was the first time in his long history of public service that he'd attended a meeting where nobody wanted something from him! He was certain that the same applied to our other guests as well.

Despite the fact that few, if any, of those who'd accepted our invitation to attend were Christians, they were all happy to be prayed for publicly. We prayed for their families and personal lives and were surprised at how open some were. The human side of their public persona consistently showed as they opened up about challenges and pressures they were experiencing.

One member of our core group, Marijke Hoek, was so inspired by the evening that she immediately began to pray that God would show her how she could create more opportunities for more Christians to pray for their own local MP. Within a few weeks she'd organised a prayer breakfast for the MP in her constituency, to which she invited two representatives from each of the churches in that area. The breakfast was very well attended and was another expression of dynamic Christian unity. All the church people who came willingly put their differences to one side in order to unite in prayer for their Member of Parliament, who, in turn, spoke warmly of the experience and has readily attended many more since then.

Marijke went on to organise similar breakfasts all around the city and is still doing so today. One MP spoke about the backbiting and jealousies she had to struggle with because she had progressed quite rapidly up the political ladder. She asked us to pray about the excessive press attention which was affecting her family as well as herself. She was adamant that she had no religious faith of any sort but added that she thought the values of Jesus were sound and strong; she had learned about him as a child and had built her own worldview on them! She, too, was more than happy to receive prayer and, more than once, I spotted her reaching for a tissue as we brought her needs before the Lord.

The most remarkable aspect of all of these gatherings is the atmosphere of openness and honesty that permeates them. You get the impression that the MP feels really safe, and even that this may be the only time they ever get the chance to share such personal and sensitive details about their lives.

God's timing

We were always aware of huge issues around the world that carried greater significance than those to which we were giving our attention in 'our own backyard': wars, famines, natural disasters and grave injustices of every kind constantly clamour for our attention until many Christians end up not praying about anything because they feel overwhelmed. Despite often feeling guilty that we were ignoring the needs of the wider world, we continued to keep our focus on our city and its immediate needs, and this meant that we consciously wore spiritual blinkers when it came to considering our next theme. You have to accept that you can't pray in a meaningful way for every issue; God had called us to pray for Manchester and we were doing our best to remain faithful to that call.

Nevertheless, there were a couple of occasions when God overruled. As we shared our ideas and began to pray, the Holy Spirit steered us in a new direction, lifting our eyes from the needs of our city to bigger issues that needed our prayers. To this day, none of us can explain how or why we found ourselves deviating so strongly from our usual pattern, but, at the time, we all agreed that God was responsible, such was the sense of accord between us. Why other huge global issues didn't stand out in the same way to us we still can't work out. His ways are not our ways; we simply followed his lead when it was so very clear to all of us.

One of these wider issues was the long-running unrest in Northern Ireland. It was around the time of the Good Friday peace agreement in 1998. During the three preceding years, three very significant events had occurred. On Saturday the

15th June 1996, at a peak shopping time the day before Father's Day, a 3,000-pound IRA bomb exploded in Manchester, injuring more than 200 people and ripping into the fabric of the main shopping centre. It is generally believed that this was motivated by Republican frustration at the lack of progress being made by the Government in the long-running peace talks in Northern Ireland.

Less than a year later, in 1997, the British Government changed hands and within its first year, the Good Friday Agreement was reached. A remarkable feature of this agreement was the cross-party support it received, both in Northern Ireland and here in England. Outgoing and incoming Government ministers co-operated fully to ensure that the momentum and goodwill that had accrued was not hindered by party politics or changes of personnel, and regular high-profile talks were held between Tony Blair and Bertie Ahern. The agreement was embraced by the people of Northern Ireland, who voted to accept it in a referendum, albeit by a narrow majority.

It seemed to us that God had his hand quite firmly on this process, and we sensed that he was calling Christians around the world to pray that it would hold, at least to give sufficient time for the formation of the new Northern Ireland Assembly.

The Good Friday Agreement was, without doubt, the most encouraging breakthrough in the history of The Troubles that any of us could recall. We decided to abandon our original plans for the July gathering in 1998 and turn our attention instead to praying for peace in Northern Ireland.

We chose the cathedral in the city centre as our venue: it stands just yards away from where the bomb exploded and still bore the scars. We invited groups of Christians from Northern

93

Ireland to join us, both Protestants and Roman Catholics, and held a memorable and moving evening of prayer with people packed into every pew.

We had a banner made for the occasion in the shape of the whole island of Ireland with a lamb sitting serenely at its centre. A subtle trickle of red flowed from the animal's side and separated into rivers running to the North and South. We presented the banner to David McCarthy, the then Secretary of the Evangelical Alliance in Northern Ireland, and a prophetic word was given that read:

> In this land of flags I am raising the flag of the kingdom and on this flag is the emblem of the lamb who was slain. It is an emblem of power. A humble lamb with a deep wound. White of wool and red of blood. Here is the renewal of the kingdom of God. I am raising this flag higher in these days and you can march under this banner with boldness and authority. The power of my kingdom is a power under submission. Walk with confidence. Your true citizenship is in heaven.

The banner is now on display at St Anne's Cathedral in Belfast.

Nine-eleven

The second major shift of focus came in 2001 when we felt it was right to give our regular quarterly Prayer Network evening to pray for the people of New York in the wake of the terrorist attacks of the 11th September 2001. We'd already held a special extra evening of prayer just a few days after that day that will be forever etched in everyone's memory. However, as we met later in the year to plan for our regular January event, we felt that we just couldn't move straight back to 'business as usual'. God was again calling us to lift our gaze and pray for others whose need was more urgent than ours.

94

One of our regular police contacts, Supt Neil Wain, had been in New York giving some training to the NYPD when the attack on the twin towers happened. He'd stayed there longer than originally planned to help provide pastoral care to the many police officers involved in dealing with what was easily the most traumatic event in recent American history. Some of these women and men had not slept for days as they toiled away at the rubble searching for survivors. Day turned to night and back again to day as thousands of bereaved and disoriented people swarmed around Ground Zero desperately hoping for miracles.

The police and other emergency services' personnel cried with them and gave themselves ceaselessly to care for them. As a result, many became deeply affected psychologically, and Neil and other Christian police officers were able to lead a number of their colleagues to faith in Christ.

Through Neil, we invited a group of these Christian officers to fly over from New York and take part in the evening. It was a great privilege for us to give one of our regular gatherings over to share with them in their grief and stand with them in prayer. One by one they testified to the sustaining power of God in their own lives and recounted story upon story of colleagues giving their lives to the Lord in the aftermath of the tragedy.

By the end of the evening, the atmosphere had changed dramatically. The cloud of mourning that had weighed so heavily on us all at the outset had been burned away by the brightness of the truth and power of the gospel. Jesus was still Lord. His purposes would not be thwarted by a terrorist attack, no matter how devastating or chilling. We left the building arm in arm with our new friends, tearstains on our faces and yet a song of praise on our lips. God is good! All the time!

five

a marriage made in heaven

Debra

Come on! Let's pray!

Our good friend Andy Hawthorne is one of those rare people who will happily own up to being a lifelong learner. During his amazingly fruitful ministry as an evangelist and as a key leader in the church in Manchester God has taught Andy many things, including the importance of prayer in the context of mission.

He regularly preaches that the two need to go hand in hand and, with characteristic bluntness and vulnerability, insists that mission without prayer is almost certainly a waste of time and effort! On the other hand, he argues, prayer that never even leans towards the needs of the lost can be in danger of becoming self-indulgent and out of step completely with God's plans for the world. Thankfully, he doesn't just preach about prayer; he prays as well, all the time!

Over the years, Andy's influence considerably shaped the way we organised prayer gatherings, making us increasingly aware of the need to ensure that our prayers were constantly in line with God's desire to transform society through proclamation and presence. His almost obsessive outward focus on lost people constantly pulled us towards the real needs of our city, so that our meetings have never been allowed to become inwardly oriented on church issues (which often happens when groups of Christians put their hands together and close their eyes …).

As well as influencing us, Andy often comments that his participation in Prayer Network over the years has sharpened his own commitment to bathe in prayer every aspect of his work with The Message.

Both Frank and I have spent more hours than we can count in meetings of various kinds with Andy and others, and neither of us can recall any that didn't start and finish with Andy saying, 'Come on, let's pray!' Every working day in The Message offices starts with a half-hour prayer meeting. Once a week that's extended to an hour, and once a month everything stops for a whole day as everyone disappears for a prayer retreat together: performers, evangelists, administrators, technical operators, managers and directors. The whole team draws aside from the busyness of earth to refocus on the business of heaven. Message employees even have a clause in their contract that insists that they attend at least one major prayer event per month! That must be unique; I wonder if anyone has ever been sacked for not doing so!

The youth of today

Our first contact with The Message (or Message To Schools, as it was called in those days) was way back in 1988 when Frank and I took our youth group along to the special evangelistic weekend that is now a landmark in the spiritual history of our city, The Message 88.

The impact on our youngsters was profound. Many of them were converted and all were impressed by the clear and relevant way the gospel was presented through music, drama, testimony and no-nonsense preaching in a language they understood.

We kept in touch and became friends with Andy and his wife, Michelle, both of whom were regulars at just about every Prayer Network event from the beginning. They were fully in agreement with our vision to reach the whole city through prayer and liked the way we ran our meetings – perhaps mainly because there was always a good number of young people present, not the norm for most prayer meetings in those days.

We often reflect on one of our most memorable Prayer Network events when the theme was young people and schools. It took place in September 1998 at the impressive three-storey building belonging to the King's Church in the city centre. The main meeting-room on the middle floor seats around 800, and it was full to overflowing on this occasion. We got to the point in our running order where we were going to pray for Christian schools workers and we decided to ask any present to come forward for prayer. We stressed that we wanted only those who were full time, thinking that there may be a dozen or so. We were totally amazed when over 100 came forward! Rapturous applause broke out to honour and appreciate these dedicated missionaries.

We went along the line asking each one where they were based and who they worked for. Twenty-five or so were with Pais, a dynamic organisation led by Paul Gibbs (a young Assemblies of God pastor with a passion for training and releasing young people into evangelism in schools; Paul had also been involved in the 1988 Message event and started Pais largely as a result of being inspired by it). Some worked for Scripture Union, Covenanters, Urban Action, Youth for Christ and others. Well over half were involved in the recently formed Eden Partnerships started by The Message.

It was encouraging to see so many fired-up young men and women giving their lives to make Christ known to children at school. One man, Paul Morley, whose ministry includes some stunning illusions that enthral young people as he explains the gospel, stepped up to the microphone. He revealed that, around ten years earlier, there were only three full-time Christian schools workers in the whole of Manchester. Was God doing something special in our city, or what?!

Millennium fever

Around this time, everyone was talking about the imminent date change. Not only were we facing the turn of a century, a momentous event in itself, but also the turn of the Millennium – an almost unimaginable concept for most people.

London's controversial Dome was taking shape; IT experts all around the globe were warning computer users to prepare for the mother of all electronic bugs, and soothsayers were predicting the end of the world.

Some Christians thought the Saviour might well return in the year 2000 and so were preparing either to be 'caught up in the air' with him or to begin their new existence as co-rulers of the earth alongside him. Christian bookshops did a roaring trade in End Time titles, and the Christian press had an unusually easy time filling their Letters to the Editor sections.

There were, thankfully, more than enough people who preferred to party rather than panic as one Millennium prepared to give way to another – and plenty of Christians who wanted to use this once-in-fifteen-lifetimes opportunity to celebrate and communicate the good news. Manchester's believers were soon to be challenged to channel their millennial energies into the 'biggest mission the city has ever seen' (most of Andy's advance vision statements include the word 'biggest'!): Soul Survivor–The Message 2000 (SSM2K). And Prayer Network was to have a strategic role to play, both in the preparation stages and during the days of the mission itself.

SSM2K started life in the creative mind of Andy Hawthorne as nothing more than a dream. He visualised literally thousands of young people from all over the world coming to Manchester for a week or two in the summer of 2000 to join forces in proclaiming the gospel through creative and youth-friendly means. There would be Bible teaching in the mornings, big music events in the evenings, and the afternoons would see the city flooded with teams of youngsters eagerly engaged in outreach projects of various kinds.

Initially, the plan was to accommodate these urban mission-aries on the floors of church buildings, or maybe in university halls of residence, although both options turned out to be impractical in the end.

As the 1990s rolled on, Andy's dream began to crystallise and a solid vision was birthed during a meeting with Mike Pilavachi, who heads up Soul Survivor. The two of them devised an exciting plan to relocate Soul Survivor, the success-ful annual summer youth and student festival of worship, teaching and ministry, from the idyllic tranquillity of Shepton Mallet to the urban sprawl of Manchester. Mike joked that he'd got bored with evangelising sheep for the last few years and it was time to hit the streets and share the good news with some real people.

The delegates would camp in Heaton Park, one of Manches-ter's largest recreational areas, situated on the north side of the city. The tent-city atmosphere of a normal Soul Survivor festival would be preserved and the added dimension of outreach would make the whole thing a real adventure for the thousands who would come. It promised to be a memorable way to mark the Millennium and quickly became an inspiring vision that Mike and Andy enthused about on their travels around the UK and overseas.

The year 2000 was to be the seventh year since Prayer Network began and as we started to work closely with Andy to plan the preparation stages we remembered how the number seven had been spoken prophetically over us at one of our earliest gatherings. We still didn't know exactly what it meant, but felt sure that seven years of inter-church, city-wide prayer leading up to such a large-scale venture must be a good sign that God was going to do great things. And so we decided to make the mission the focus of all our prayer meetings for the whole of the build-up year, not realising at that stage how strategic our partnership with The Message would become in future years.

Jumpin' in the house of God

Our quarterly Prayer Network meetings were continuing to attract large numbers from across a wide range of church traditions and across the age spectrum. Once we started to partner with The Message, however, even more young people began turning up, and the whole feel of the evenings changed significantly.

Our format was already dynamic and the prayer slots, interspersed with interviews and information, were focused and specific, giving the evening a sense of pace and direction. Now, though, we found ourselves moving even more quickly through the programme and adding yet more variety to heighten the interest and maintain the attention of our younger prayer warriors.

Sometimes we would feature a performance slot by The Tribe during the evening; but not every time; we never advertised that they would even be attending because we didn't want to attract people for the wrong reasons. One of our core values was that we wouldn't use any well-known special guests as a draw; we only wanted people who were keen to pray. When The Tribe did come, though, they always participated in the whole evening like everyone else. They would usually spread out and sit in different parts of the auditorium, joining in with the worship and the prayers and generally being excellent role models to young and old alike.

This provided yet another opportunity for Christians to experience new ways of praying and to learn from one another. The sight, for example, of hundreds of 30-, 40- and 50-somethings pogoing for Jesus to the latest Tribe song alongside their far more able-bodied younger spiritual siblings is something to behold! Such an occurrence became commonplace as the whole church family took on the responsibility of praying for the forthcoming event.

Equally, the teenagers and 20-somethings were happy to participate in the less physically demanding times of prayer that came more naturally to their elders. One 14-year-old boy told us, 'I used to think that prayer was always boring but now I enjoy it, especially when everything goes really quiet and it feels like Jesus is actually there with you: it's mint!'

Prayer walls

During the preparation year for SSM2K, Sharon Britton, an intercessor friend, came up with the idea of providing round-the-clock prayer cover for the city. There really was so much to pray about in the build-up that this seemed an excellent way of making sure the intercession burden was shared widely, and the very idea of uninterrupted prayer was certainly inspiring. We knew that the eighteenth-century Moravians kept a constant prayer relay going for over 100 years and so it seemed at least possible that we could manage it for one year.

The idea was to have people praying for one hour at a specific time on a set day of the week. As they completed their hour they would telephone the person who was next on the rota and remind them that it was their turn. Also, specific requests could be passed on in this way, meaning that urgent matters didn't get missed. Once the 168 hours of a week were taken we would have a wall of prayer around the city.

Sharon got to work producing sign-up cards and charts, and we soon had so many volunteers that we had to create a second 'wall'. This proved to be a really effective method of enabling prevailing prayer, although, for some, the experience of stumbling around a dark bedroom at three o' clock in the morning in search of a ringing mobile is not one that will be cherished! The idea that picking the slot no one wants will bring some kind of spiritual reward is entirely spurious!

It was around this time that I first had the idea of using email to send regular prayer bulletins. Although it now seems as though we've all been using electronic means of communication for donkey's years, the truth is that, even a few years ago, it was a novelty that some thought would be a passing fad like the Rubik's cube. In truth, email is a gift to prayer co-ordinators! Instead of spending hours (and large amounts of cash) printing prayer lists and stuffing and stamping envelopes, we could now press a few computer keys and know that hundreds of people would get the information within seconds. Once a month we sent a comprehensive list of all the latest prayer needs relating to the mission and often urgent one-off requests were sent electronically as well.

Specific prayers

Once the mission was underway, some of the prayer needs became very specific indeed, such as a list of building materials required for one of the outreach projects that involved turning a piece of wasteland into a play area: 20 m curbing; 4,000 white bricks; 100 l blue paint; 20 m^3 concrete! Within days, every item on the list had been donated by local companies.

As well as asking God to save people, we prayed for lawnmowers, skips, topsoil and wheelbarrows, and through the growing network of praying Christians, answers were celebrated on a daily basis. It's difficult to imagine, looking back a few years, how anyone ever managed without email, but at the time, this was a truly revolutionary approach to keeping the prayer fires fuelled.

One major prayer request kept on recurring on our prayer bulletins: 10,000 ft^2 empty building in the city centre, as close as possible to the MEN Arena. Talk about praying specifically! It was the height of the skateboard boom, and Andy was adamant that the mission must include a free skate park that would attract hundreds of unchurched kids. It would be run by Christian volunteers who spoke the same language and shared the same passion for collecting bruises while doing high-speed gymnastics on small wooden wheelbases!

As the big event approached, the lack of a suitable venue for the skate park was one of our major concerns. Our son, Josh, who was eleven at the time and a dedicated skateboarder, came across a printout of one of our prayer bulletins and asked us whether it would help if he prayed as well; he genuinely wasn't sure if the prayers of a young guy with an obvious vested interest would count!

We encouraged him to add his prayers to the many that were already happening and, guess what? Within a week, a businessman who owned an empty warehouse just a stone's throw from the Arena, contacted Andy and offered its free use not only for the duration of the mission but for a few months following as well! Praise God, and well done Josh!

The mother of all prayer meetings

As the build-up to SSM2K entered its final month, we were looking forward to what we felt sure would be the largest prayer meeting our city had ever seen. We booked one of Manchester's biggest concert venues, the Apollo Theatre, more used to playing host to thousands of screaming pop fans than doubling as a house of prayer, and held our breath.

We needed at least 1,000 people to turn up to make it work (not to mention the £8,000 we would need in the offering to pay the bills). Amazingly, for some reason, Frank's characteristic pessimism didn't kick in on this occasion. Even he was full of faith that God would honour our confidence in him. And he wasn't wrong.

On Wednesday the 5th July 2000, the Apollo opened its doors to a fairly typical looking throng of customers, some of whom had queued for hours to get the best seats. The big difference, though, was that these people had turned out not to be entertained but to pray. What an occasion! There were only 23 days until the kick off, and excitement was high all across the region.

Outside the theatre, on the big display sign that normally bore the name of the current performing band, the words 'Prayer Meeting' must have caused a few raised eyebrows among the hordes of passing commuters as they streamed home along the A6, one of the city's busiest trunk roads.

Inside, the atmosphere was charged with expectancy as just under 2,000 people from the broadest possible range of Christian backgrounds lifted their voices together in a hymn of praise to start the evening. After an amazing time of worship, we welcomed a host of different people taking part in the mission, interviewed them briefly and waded into prayer for the many loose strands and gaping holes that still remained even though the project was entering its final stages.

We were still a long way short of our target to recruit 200 partner churches. Despite numerous mailshots and telephone campaigns over the last 18 months, there were still churches claiming they'd heard nothing about the mission! It was crucial that we involved as many churches as possible to develop long-term relationships in local communities where outreach projects were happening, so we prayed earnestly for more.

We had a target of 400 social action outreach projects that needed to be in place before day one of the mission, and we were nowhere near reaching it! We prayed that God would spur people on in their local areas to come up with ideas and plans in what seemed like an impossible timescale.

The police had asked if we could try to organise one especially large project which they could partner in a high-profile way. They particularly wanted it to be on a really tough estate somewhere to help them build some bridges in the context of a community where they were traditionally unwelcome. Andy wanted to allocate a team of 1,000 delegates to this, and we prayed that God would guide those involved to the right place and enable the necessary negotiations to progress swiftly and smoothly.

In typical Christian fashion, delegates were leaving it late to book, and we still needed thousands to do so in the next few weeks in order to make the whole thing viable. We prayed that youth groups would suddenly develop a sense of urgency and that those who were still undecided would make their minds up and get their bookings in quickly.

Cash flow was a major issue, especially for Soul Survivor, which relied heavily on income from its annual festival and whose trustees were exercising major levels of faith in agreeing to participate in such a departure from their usual model. We prayed that individuals would be prompted to give towards the target budget of £1,250,000 (at this point, the shortfall was around £350,000!), that partner churches would honour their pledges and that their treasurers would hurry up and sign cheques!

Five hundred adult volunteers were needed to help counsel the large numbers of young people that would respond each day. Hundreds were also needed to act as guides and travel with the groups of youngsters as they moved around the city to and from the outreach projects. We prayed that God would stir the hearts of mature believers and challenge them to give their time and energy, and that he would prevent unsuitable people from applying.

The potential for things to go wrong during the mission was huge, especially given that thousands of youngsters would be descending on a big city they didn't know, camping out in a public park, moving around in and out of some of the country's most socially challenged estates with little more than a few angels to protect them from harm! We prayed a great deal for the safety and well-being of the delegates and that their families back home would know the peace of God in their hearts.

As the evening progressed there was a growing sense that God was hearing and answering all our prayers. Each time we broke into groups to pray, you could hear the volume rise as faith increased and God's people interceded with mounting confidence and fervour. It truly was an awesome evening, with

Christians from across the region all standing together in unity and getting fully behind this exciting mission in prayer. God's presence was powerfully felt and his people were blessed. We left the Apollo with a sense of anticipation and confidence. God's seal of approval was clearly on the mission – the evening of prayer had confirmed that for us all. His agenda was being served and his name was being glorified. Hallelujah!

Behind the scenes

As the big event approached, we started to think about how we could keep prayer going during the mission itself. Andy really does believe that prayer is the most vital aspect of mission, and he urged me to find ways of sustaining the prayer momentum we'd built up through the year for the duration of SSM2K.

Together, we came up with a two-pronged approach. We would set aside a large tent on the campsite where delegates could go and pray at any time during the day or night. This would be looked after by Rachel and Gordon Hickson, who had worked with Mike Pilavachi at Soul Survivor for many years. It was the very early days of the international 24/7 Prayer Movement led by Pete Greig, and the idea of round-the-clock prayer was spreading like wildfire. A ten-day mission like this was the ideal place to set up a round-the-clock prayer centre.

As soon as we got access to the site at Heaton Park, a group of Manchester students transformed the cavernous emptiness of a marquee into a welcoming house of prayer by creating a ceiling of criss-crossed ropes, over which they draped sheets to create internal walls. Hundreds of cushions were imported to make the coconut-matting floor more comfortable, and the finished product served well as a 24/7 prayer base for the duration of the mission. Each time I popped in there were people praying (as well as some snoring!), usually in small groups, sometimes with candles burning, sometimes with music playing, always with lists of people they'd met during the outreach afternoons. As the mission progressed, the sheets became increasingly covered with holy graffiti and pinned-on prayers and the sense of God's presence in the tent became almost tangible. It felt like walking into a cathedral to me. That sense of awe and wonder you feel when your eyes are drawn to the splendour of the architecture and the beauty of the art was equally present in spite of the humility of the environment. I wondered if this was how it might have felt for the shepherds in the stable of the Nativity, a lowly yet holy space. It was a real encouragement to know that the mission was bathed in prayer by the delegates themselves. So often, Christian events seem to slip into an entertainment mode that loses sight of the reality of the spiritual realm. Not so for this one. SSM2K was soaked in prayer from start to finish.

As well as enabling prayer in tent-city, we decided to hold a nightly prayer meeting in a church building in the city centre. This would run concurrently with the evening outreach event at the *Manchester Evening News* Arena and would be open to anyone and everyone, especially Christians from all around Manchester who were not going to attend the big nights at the Arena. We called this the Engine Room, thinking about the unseen yet vital area of a ship, where people work flat out to keep the fires burning that generate the power to keep the vessel moving.

Each night, we asked a different church to lead the Engine Room meeting, providing a worship band and an MC. We prayed for all the urgent issues that arose, such as a sudden computer crash experienced by the Soul Survivor admin team and the various health issues affecting key people on a daily basis: there were sore throats, minor injuries and one or two serious cases that needed hospital treatment.

Most evenings we were visited by artists and speakers who were taking part at the Arena. They appreciated being prayed for, and many came back on their nights off to join with us in prayer for the success of the mission.

SSM2K broke a number of moulds. It wasn't only enormously fruitful in terms of hundreds of teenagers coming to faith, but it also had a huge impact on whole communities, the hundreds of care projects speaking loudly about the love of God without using words. Partnering with the police was another novel and rewarding dimension which Frank will expand upon in Chapter 7.

For me, it was particularly thrilling to see prayer taken so seriously and valued so highly by evangelists. The partnership between Prayer Network and The Message had proved to be really effective, and it was clear that God had plans for more of the same in the years ahead.

six
multiplication

Debra

Into orbit

I don't know why it is that God sometimes chooses to speak to people in a rather oblique way. In my case, it usually starts with a single word popping into my head, often while I'm driving, which may explain why I get lost so frequently. Instead of concentrating on following directions and road signs, I find myself driving on autopilot and using my conscious mind to mull over what God might be trying to say to me!

This is exactly what happened one day back in 1997 as I was heading home after a meeting with a church leader in Rochdale, one of Greater Manchester's outlying towns. Out of nowhere, the word 'satellite' interrupted my navigational thought process in such a sharp and clear way that I actually spoke it out loud at the same time (missing the turning for the M60 as a result!).

Satellite is not a word I would normally use in everyday conversation. I knew that satellites were things that spun around in space and took pictures of earth, and that they were partly responsible for the increase in televised football but, beyond that, the word meant nothing to me. So, I spent the next half-hour switching between trying to find a new way home without using the motorway and praying for further revelation.

By the time I got home I thought I'd got it. 'Satellite towns!' I exclaimed out loud as I walked into the house. I knew I'd heard the phrase used to refer to the towns that surround a big city. On the map they look as though they're in orbit around a large planet. Towns like Rochdale, Oldham, Stockport and so on were satellites to Manchester. God was speaking about how we were to include them in our city-reaching strategy. I was excited at the prospect of another new phase opening up and couldn't wait to get on with praying it through and making it happen.

Far and wide

Since we'd started to call churches together to pray for the city there had always been a few uncertainties about whether Christians from Greater Manchester's surrounding towns should be included in the outworking of our vision.

One of the reasons for this concerned the redrawing of local government boundaries in the 1980s. Prior to this, there was a clearly defined geographical area called Greater Manchester that was governed by Greater Manchester Council. This included the dozens of smaller towns that now make up the ten boroughs of Manchester, Salford, Bolton, Bury, Oldham, Rochdale, Stockport, Tameside, Trafford and Wigan.

We decided from the start to make our prayer gatherings known right across the conurbation and there were always groups that came to join us from far and wide. In some areas, though, I'd encountered strong resistance to the idea of travelling 10 or 20 miles into the city centre, especially in areas with a strong local identity. 'Why pray for Manchester?' some would ask, almost indignantly, 'We're not in Manchester; our focus is on our own town.'

This was quite understandable as well, since some of these population centres are almost cities in their own right (Salford actually is a city; Bolton will probably be awarded city status soon), with their own council, cathedral, well-known football team, university and so on. We'd never suggested that anyone should get involved if they felt this way but we'd always given them the option. Living in close proximity to a city of Manchester's significance seemed reason enough for many to join with us to pray for the specific relevant issues. Others, though, felt that they had enough to pray for just in terms of their immediate locality.

To maintain the balance between local and regional emphases, we always tried to apply our prayer sessions to both levels. Often, this was the logical way to break down our numbers during an evening. When praying for local government, for example, we asked people to move to different parts of the auditorium and stand together with others from their own borough. When praying for healthcare, we did the same with local hospitals.

It was on occasions like these that a pattern became clear – some 'satellites' were consistently strongly represented, such as Salford and Stockport, while numbers from others were always low. Perhaps distance was the main reason for this, since to travel from Wigan, Bolton or Rochdale, for example, does take twice as long as from Stockport or Salford. Whatever the reason, we'd always just accepted the fact and got on with things regardless: after all, we did have a huge number of people from all across the region gathering to pray. It wasn't as though God was going to withhold his blessing from one particular town just because only a handful had turned up from there!

Planting out

But now this was about to change. As I prayed into the satellite concept, I began to sense God saying that he wanted to see the same sort of regular prayer events in these surrounding areas. He was calling me to help enable leaders in these different places to replicate what we were doing in Manchester.

The vision gradually became sharp and clear in my mind: ten Prayer Networks in the ten boroughs of Greater Manchester, each focused on its immediate locality, gathering quarterly to pray into different 'pillars of society'; each praying for spiritual breakthrough in their own population centre; each drawing together churches from diverse backgrounds to celebrate their unity in Christ and take a powerful first step in seeing their area transformed for his glory! And, once a year we could all join together to share the burden of praying for the great city of Manchester which plays such an important role in the economic and social well-being of all its surrounding boroughs.

The obvious place to begin was Rochdale because one member of our core group, David Corke, was the leader of Hebron Church in the town. As well as sharing our vision for city-wide prayer and co-operation, David and his wife, Carol, had a passion to see churches working together in their own area. They were thrilled at the prospect of starting a local Prayer Network and set to work to recruit some like-minded leaders.

They stuck to the principles of Radical Middle Ground and looked for people from a broad range of church-style and background who shared the same values of relational unity and kingdom priority. Their core group came together quickly and they held their launch meeting at a packed Champness Hall, a well-known concert venue in the town centre in 1998.

Oldham followed soon after, with united prayer gatherings springing up all around the town. Church leaders grew closer together over the next few years as the barriers came down between them. They were able to speak with one voice to the media during the race riots of May 2001, expressing acceptance and love to Muslims in the name of Jesus Christ. The sense of unity in Oldham enabled The Message trust to plant a new Eden Partnership project on the notorious Fitton Hill estate in 2003, through which many young people have found Christ.

Next was Stockport. Their launch meeting was attended by over 200, most of whom had never been to a Prayer Network gathering before, including the Chief Executive of Stockport Borough Council.

Prayer walking became a regular feature of the Stockport group; one of their local Christian police officers, Chief Superintendent Neil Wain, loves to tell the story of how he took a group of his colleagues out on the streets late one Friday night. His intention was to show them how violent and dangerous Stockport can be, especially at the weekend in the town centre, but, despite combing all the usual trouble spots throughout the entire night, they couldn't find even the slightest hint of anything resembling crime.

He hadn't realised that one of his colleagues, Superintendent Val Binsted, had been out prayer walking the night before with Stockport Prayer Network, around the usually troubled town centre. It turned out to be the only totally crime-free Friday night that anyone in the local force could remember! A great testimony to the power of prayer, but also a challenge to Christians everywhere to do much more.

More doors open

God opened door after door for me as I contacted people in each of the ten boroughs of Greater Manchester. In every area there was someone who'd caught the vision already by coming to one of our main meetings. Many of them had been praying for their own local expression of something similar to the central Manchester model and, in some cases, had begun to gather a few leaders together as a starting-point.

One such place was Tameside (a borough that includes nine towns to the east of Manchester: Ashton, Denton, Droylsden, Hattersley, Hyde, Longdendale, Mossley, Mottram and Staly-bridge). There hadn't been any kind of co-operation between churches in this area for as long as anyone could remember but God was on the move and things were changing.

The first Tameside Prayer Network meeting was launched on the 24th October 2000 at Mottram Evangelical Church, which would become the host church for another Eden Partnership a couple of years later aimed at reaching out to the notorious Hattersley Estate. Incidentally, this particular Eden was recently featured in a very hostile TV documentary broadcast by the BBC. As a result, the Eden workers were refused admission to schools for a time and local authorities withdrew their support. However, after much concerted prayer, the situation has totally reversed and the Hattersley Eden Partnership is now one of the most fruitful in the whole of the city.

It won't work here!

The large town of Bolton has a strong tradition of church co-operation in its past, but by the end of the millennium things had cooled considerably. When I first got in touch with a couple of local church leaders I was greeted with a distinct lack of enthusiasm. 'Churches just don't get together,' I was told. 'Leaders are suspicious of each other's motives and protective of their people.' Now, where had I heard that before?!

I wasn't going to be put off by a couple of negative comments and kept searching for the right contact. Eventually I came across Rob Coleman, a really solid guy who was leading a new church plant in the area. I never would have thought that someone leading a brand new church would be able to put other church leaders at ease, let alone inspire them to work together, but Rob's warm character and non-threatening style seemed to do the trick. He genuinely believes that the advance of God's kingdom is more important than counting heads on a Sunday morning, and his quiet, thoughtful approach gave others the confidence to work with him.

He gathered a few other leaders who shared the same heart to work together and Bolton Prayer Network was born. Their launch meeting took place in July 1999 at Claremont Church in the town centre, taking the theme of young people as their focus. SSM2K was a year away, and plans were just coming together to make Bolton a key region in the build-up phase.

In October 2000, they held a memorable event, which took the theme of homelessness and, perhaps not surprisingly, several homeless people turned up. Jeff Smethurst, the Assistant Director of Housing for Bolton Council, spoke about the issues challenging the local authority. There were then officially 1,200 homeless people in Bolton, and many more who were not officially registered. Jeff said that the council was reliant on voluntary organisations for help, particularly the church. Christian organisations like Urban Outreach were doing a fantastic job in providing short-term accommodation. Winter Watch raised £4,000 by a sponsored bike ride to open a winter shelter, and the local Salvation Army were housing 72 homeless people in their hostel. It was great to hear the church being thanked and praised by the local authority.

A twin-twin scenario

Trafford Prayer Network was launched in November 2001. Around 150 people from 10 different churches turned out to pray for the borough. The Mayor of Trafford (Harry Faulkner) was invited and when asked how local Christians could pray for him he shared that he wanted to see Trafford twinned with the Ugandan city of Jinja to build on and broaden the links that Altrincham Baptist Church had recently started to forge by sending mission teams there. The big problem was that Trafford had a policy of not twinning with other cities (no one really knows why) and he couldn't see a way around this. He had vowed to visit Jinja at his own expense if necessary and to find some way of forging an official connection of some sort.

Within a year, God answered these prayers convincingly: Trafford softened their stance, paid for Harry's visit and agreed to create an Official Friendship Link with Jinja – a brand-new model of twinning that allowed them to bend the rules for the only time in their history! Since then, the links have grown stronger and Trafford Education Authority has designated the Ugandan city as a core component of its primary school curriculum, and is also working towards an official partnership with the Jinja Education Authority.

Trafford is a huge area that takes in very diverse communities like wealthy Hale and Altrincham on the one hand and inner-city Old Trafford on the other. Historically, the borough has always been defined as North Trafford and South Trafford, reinforcing the suburb versus inner-city divide. The establishing of a single Prayer Network across the whole area was a strong, prophetic symbol of unity and although it continues to be a

120

challenge to draw people together from both areas, the core group is determined that this beacon of oneness should remain in place.

Stomping ground

One borough that's very special to Frank and me is Salford. Frank was born there and spent the first few years of his life training to be a juvenile delinquent in the cobbled labyrinth of alleyways and backyards. When the Corrie credits roll on TV, he loves to point to the old terraced houses and remind us all that the programme's first episodes were actually shot just around the corner from his home.

My fondness for Salford has only come about in recent years, and is largely to do with the warmth and generosity of the people I've met and worked with there. We've made some very special friends in Salford and seen God do great things in changing the spiritual climate in parallel with the gradual but substantial physical regeneration that's happening there.

Salford is a city with a proud history of growth and industrial significance. In the nineteenth century, its population grew from 12,000 to 250,000, and it became one of Britain's largest boroughs, receiving city status in 1926.

In the last decade of the twentieth century, Salford gained more new jobs than any other region of Greater Manchester and became one of Europe's prime examples of urban regeneration, with Salford Quays and the Lowry Centre standing out as stunning symbols of the new life emerging there.

Northern hospitality

The most frequent comment you'll hear made by visitors to Salford is almost certain to be about how welcoming and friendly the local people are. Like many northern cities where life has been tough for most, the natives have developed a way of dealing with difficulties that demands a positive outlook and a community spirit.

Consequently, establishing Salford Prayer Network was not only effortless for me but also a really enjoyable phase of my life. I was welcomed to the initial discussions like a member of the Royal Family! Malcolm Lane, one of the prime movers, introduced me as representing 'the best thing that's happened' during his time in the church in Manchester: how embarrassing! And at the launch in March 2000 their Info Sheet for the evening included this piece written by him under the heading 'Salford, dear to God's heart':

> 'Prayer Network – the best thing since sliced bread.' I said this recently to a group of Salford Church Leaders, and as far as the church in Greater Manchester goes, I believe Prayer Network is playing a major part in what God has planned for this area.
>
> Never before have we seen God's people coming together in such numbers to pray, to lower denominational barriers and to build protective walls of co-operation, trust and reconciliation.
>
> For some years it has been my desire to see this happen in our city of Salford as well … now, at last, Debra has seen the light and given her blessing! (Actually, we bless her for all her hard work and God-given vision.)
>
> Despite the bad press it receives, Salford is dear to God's heart and his purposes for our city will be fulfilled as his church comes together. God is up to something in Salford, and we want to be part of it!

Twenty-five different churches were represented at the launch, and all their leaders were present and prayed for. There was a strong sense of togetherness evident from the start and a positive atmosphere charged with anticipation. A youth band called Heat led the worship, and their set included a song they'd written especially for the launch, 'Beautiful One', a serenade to the city, calling it to rise from the dust and enjoy new life. They projected a map of Salford onto a screen with the boundary line clearly marked, and there were audible gasps as everyone immediately saw the clear outline of a dove! What a great way to link in to prayer for the power and presence of the Holy Spirit to come to the city.

Up and running

The Salford churches took to praying together like an umbrella to the local weather. They extended acceptance and grace readily and preferred one another in love with ease. They quickly got into their stride and began to cover the same themes that we'd followed in central Manchester, requesting guidance and support from me that I was only too happy to give.

They started their own Leaders' Lunch, which immediately flourished and is still going strong today, and they gave the new Eden Partnership on the Langworthy Estate their wholehearted support.

Four years on, their enthusiasm for prayer has grown and we regularly hear of some new initiative. Just recently, a special week of prayer for Salford took place, launched with a big meeting, attended by the mayor, that filled the Civic Centre to overflowing. During the week, groups prayed in various official locations, including the Education Directorate and the police station. Jill Baker, Director of Education and Leisure for Salford said:

'Most people working in local government acknowledge that the only way we are going to see communities transformed is through strong partnerships between statutory and voluntary sector agencies. In Salford, I believe that we have seen some very positive results from partnership working between the city council, the police and local churches. I am personally greatly encouraged to know that council services and council workers are being supported by Christians who feel that prayer and action make a difference to communities. The week of prayer in Salford focused people's minds on the needs of their communities, and I know that prayer for the city is continuing.'

Almost there

Two of the ten borough Prayer Networks are still in the process of becoming established as we write. A group of three leaders in Bury recently began to be drawn together and realised that, although their churchmanship varied greatly, each had a real heart to work with others for the sake of their town. They'd heard about the planting out of Prayer Network into other boroughs and asked me to talk to them about how to get their churches together to pray in a similar way. Like many other areas in towns and cities across the UK, Bury suffers from that strange phenomenon of extreme parochialism which actually dictates who ought to mix with whom! In this case, people from Radcliffe, a neighbouring suburb, will have nothing to do with residents of Bury itself, according to local vicar, Nick Grayshon. Nobody knows why; that's just the way it is! It's frustrating when you encounter this sort of thing, and it certainly delays the process of mobilising the church to pray for their immediate communities, but we've seen God turn round situations like this time after time.

It's a similar story in Wigan, except that there is a clearly traceable cause. Apparently, at the time of the Wars of the Roses in the latter part of the fifteenth century, the two neighbouring towns of Leigh and Wigan found themselves supporting opposite sides. Despite the passage of 500 years, there

124

remains a strong sense of division between the residents of these two towns that largely make up the borough of Wigan.

Many local Christians comment on the lack of unity even within churches, let alone between them, but there is a growing desire to see this change. Over the last few years, there have been some signs of encouragement as a small number of leaders have begun to network and pray together. Out of this came a Prayer Network style meeting at the Queen's Hall in Wigan town centre. It was a good evening and people did gather from across the Leigh/Wigan divide to pray for unity and reconciliation.

On the way home from this I got hopelessly lost (again!) and witnessed a fight between two large gangs of youths. It was so bad that my companion, Wendy, a member of our team of intercessors, called the police. Then we sat and prayed until the fight was over. We felt as though God was speaking to us about the depth of division and the strength of anger that existed in the history of the people of this borough. When the police spoke to us later they said it was fairly normal for this area. It does seem that, in some places, there is a level of hatred around that can't be dealt with by any political action or social programme – all the more need for Christians to wage war in the heavenly realms using the powerful weapons of prayer.

At the time of writing, Wendy and I have just been to Leigh to pray with a lovely Pentecostal pastor friend of mine, Yaw Adudwamaa. His church has suffered from a series of splits over many years and he and his wife, Dorothy, and their six children are working to promote unity in their own church and across the town. They're both acutely aware of the power of prayer and expect to see things change between Wigan and Leigh in the coming months. We'll stand with them and help them as much as possible, confident in the power of God to break through. My goal to see ten Prayer Networks in the ten boroughs of Greater Manchester will take a little longer than I'd originally hoped, but we're almost there!

Big picture

At the same time as stimulating more localised prayer within the boroughs of Manchester, we also felt it was important not to lose sight of our city-wide oneness. We decided to make sure that we had an annual all-inclusive prayer meeting in the central Manchester area. The boroughs would plan to host three local events each year, leaving the date in the fourth quarter free, so that any who wanted to make the trip to Manchester city centre could do so. The first of these was held in 2000 to coincide with SSM2K, as described in the previous chapter: the mother of all prayer meetings!

Each year since, we've held a similar annual event. In 2001, the city was preparing to host the Commonwealth Games so we gathered in the Velodrome, the cycling arena immediately opposite the building site that would become the City of Manchester Stadium (now the home of Frank's precious football team, Manchester City!).

Booking secular venues is always a real faith venture for me. The costs can be stunningly high but to accommodate very large numbers there simply is no alternative. Also, on this occasion, it seemed important for us to pray for the Games in a sports stadium and the Velodrome was the natural choice, given its proximity to the site of the main stadium.

I rang the manager, Jarl Walsh, who at first assumed that I wanted to book one of the smaller rooms: he did say it was the first time anyone had ever asked to book a prayer meeting there! When I said we wanted to book the whole venue he was quite surprised and a little intrigued. He said he already had another booking for the same day but he would try to switch things around to accommodate us. Next came the tricky question, how much would it cost?

'Oh I won't charge you the commercial rate,' Jarl said, which I knew was around £3,000. 'You can hire the whole venue for £300.' Absolutely amazing, especially when you consider that some churches have quoted us that sort of figure in the past!

Midsummer multitudes

It was another inspiring evening, with over 2,000 people braving a heatwave to turn out from all around the city to pray for the success of the Games. Guests included: Johnny Clay, a member of the 2000 British Olympic cycling team; representatives from the city council's Games committee, and two young cyclists who treated us to several laps around the banked wooden track while we were praying!

A BBC TV crew turned up, and our prayer meeting made the national ten o' clock news with amazing shots of huge crowds worshipping in the background as the presenter explained that thousands had turned out to pray for the Games!

One major item on the prayer agenda that night was the need for hosts to accommodate the families of athletes from around the world, many of whom could barely afford to travel to the UK let alone pay hotel bills. More Than Gold, an inter-church group specially convened to co-ordinate Christian initiatives relating to the Games, challenged Christians to offer hospitality and to use this as an opportunity to show God's love to these special visitors to our city. At the end of the evening, hundreds of available beds were registered at the Athletes' Family Hosting stand.

The city council was facing a number of challenges in the run-up to this momentous occasion, especially the need to recruit large amounts of money through sponsorship. Moreover, there seemed to be a degree of scepticism from other parts of the UK as to whether a city like Manchester had the ability to handle such a high-profile event. We prayed for God's hand to be on those carrying responsibility for these areas and, as the record now shows, the eventual outcome was a major coup for our city, with everything going well and all challenges overcome.

Transformation

The council leaders attending the evening expressed sincere appreciation to the church for the prayers they received. This in itself was a huge example of transformation: for as long as anyone could remember, not one single member of Manchester City Council had ever said anything positive about Christians; in fact, we'd always been on the receiving end of what seemed to be an overtly atheistic agenda. Perhaps this had been worsened by a perception that seemed to be commonly held, namely that Christians are defined by what they are opposed to.

We challenged everyone on the night to put aside any political preferences and to get behind the council as it worked to show the world that Manchester is a city capable of hosting an event of truly global significance. Everyone stood as we prayed for Frances Done, the chair of the Games committee. The 'Amen' was followed by a tumultuous round of applause as she left the stage with tears welling up in her eyes.

It's so exciting to see the church blessing the secular authorities, and to witness the opportunity it gives for God to show himself to people who may well have written him out of their lives. It's no exaggeration to say that the church is perceived and treated very differently in our city these days. There may well be other elements in the explanation for this but many believe that the total turnaround in attitudes can be traced directly to that auspicious evening at the Velodrome, when the power of God was so present that we could almost feel the breath of the angels on the back of our necks!

Sing hallelujah!

Just a few days later, I received a phone call from the Games committee. They wanted to know if the churches of Manchester could provide 200 singers to form a choir for the opening ceremony. What an opportunity! I immediately said yes without even thinking. On putting down the phone, though, I began to wonder how on earth I could manage this, especially as my knowledge and experience of organising choirs was zero!

Oddly, there seemed to be a thought floating around in the back of my mind that I tried to pin down. Suddenly, I remembered that Andy Silver, the new music director at Elmwood Church in Salford, had told me only a week or two earlier that he had a vision to form an inter-church choir. I phoned him there and then, and he agreed to co-ordinate the auditions and rehearsals if I would help to promote the project around the churches.

Rehearsals began within a few weeks, and everyone worked really hard. The title of the song had to be kept a big secret at the request of the Games committee, as was the identity of the star soloist: not even the choir knew who their lead singer was going to be until the opening night, although one or two could probably guess it would be the Salford-born tenor, Russell Watson.

I think the choir members will always remember being among the first to perform in the amazing new stadium to a global TV audience of millions. I watched them from afar and felt so pleased to see such a wonderful symbol of the unity that was growing in our city, taking centre stage at one of the largest events in the world.

Maintaining momentum

In 2002, we focused on the arts for our annual gathering and hired the spectacular Lowry Theatre in Salford to host the event. We celebrated the brilliance and creativity of an array of artists, mostly, but not exclusively Christians. We involved dancers, singers, actors, poets, painters, sculptors and not only prayed for them but showcased their work in the bars of the theatre, breaking the programme in the middle to allow time for people to have a drink and browse.

Our 2003 big meeting was held at the Apollo Theatre once more; this time the focus was on Festival Manchester, another Message mission that drew churches together from all around the region.

In 2004, we decided to broaden out even further and use our annual gathering to draw people together from all across the north-west. The venue was Bolton's Reebok Conference Centre – part of the Reebok Stadium, home of Premier League football club, Bolton Wanderers – and we worked not only with churches and other Christian groups from Greater Manchester, but also from Liverpool and other north-west cities and towns. We revisited our crime reduction theme and called the evening: 'Redeeming our communities – praying and policing in partnership'.

We'll say more about all three of these in Chapter 10.

Prepare the way of the Lord

Planting out Prayer Network into other areas would never have been something I would have considered had God not clearly prompted me. Yet, as I look at the amazing results, I marvel at his wisdom and strategy. Our ability to make a big impact for Jesus in a city like Manchester will always be limited by the sheer enormity of the challenge yet, when broken down into smaller chunks, the task appears far more achievable.

Andy Hawthorne recently met with Reinhard Bonnke, the German evangelist who heads up Christ for All Nations, and was very impressed by the man's focused and systematic approach to fulfilling the vision God gave him to see the whole of Africa 'washed in the blood of Jesus'. What an awesome challenge! In 1974, he began to hold large gospel meetings in Botswana and now, 30 years later, he has a map of Africa printed in all his books showing around three-quarters of the continent coloured in red. These are the countries that he and his team have 'soaked' in intensive bursts of gospel proclamation. Systematically, country by country, Reinhard is working towards his God-given goal.

As Andy looked at a picture of this map in one of Reinhard's books, God spoke to him powerfully. Instead of Africa, Andy saw Manchester, the borders not defining countries but boroughs. The vision took all of three seconds to crystallise. The Message's mission statement is: 'To give every young person in Greater Manchester repeated opportunities to accept Jesus and to find their place in a vibrant local church.' In some ways, this is as daunting a challenge as to see Africa washed in the blood of Jesus.

For 16 years, Andy and his team have been working in schools and on the streets in every corner of the region, with a great deal of fruit to show for their efforts. The impact they have made has been enormous but difficult to quantify. Now he could see a way of fulfilling the vision in a focused and systematic way, one borough at a time, until the whole area had been covered, by which time a new generation of kids would be emerging and the whole process could be repeated.

One major factor that immediately excited Andy as he began to think through the practicalities was the fact that churches were already co-operating in prayer in every single one of these ten boroughs! God had sent us in advance to prepare the way for this and other yet-to-be revealed initiatives, and the climate awaiting Andy was one not only of willingness but also of hunger to work together.

If The Message spends six months in each borough of Greater Manchester pouring all its resources into every secondary school in partnership with local churches in a targeted and strategic campaign of credible mass evangelism, what a different picture we might see as the next generation of adults arises. Especially given the foundation of focused, local prayer on which it can all be built. Once again, we step back in admiration and reflect on how God pieces together his plans. When the people of God (that is the wider family of God, across the denominations and streams) humble themselves and pray, he will come and heal their land.

seven

partners in crime...reduction!

Frank

All one in Christ

As a new Christian in the early 1980s, I remember attending an outreach event in Stockport Town Hall organised by the Christian Police Association. The fact that such an event could even exist intrigued me at the time, as my few brushes with the police during my pre-conversion life would suggest that the words Christian and police were inherently incompatible!

I was very surprised to discover that many officers are not only committed personally to Jesus Christ but also to making him known to their colleagues, and that their lives actually 'shine like stars' against the backdrop of the darkness that surrounds and permeates their work (Philippians 2:15). How wrong can you be?!

One such person was seated on the platform impressively dressed in full uniform, complete with the ribbons and pips of high rank. Sitting alongside him on a sofa was a diminutive figure, at completely the opposite end of the height spectrum and wearing civvies.

Marked as it was, however, the contrast between these two men was not restricted to their appearance. On the one hand, Robin Oake, Deputy Chief Constable of Greater Manchester Police, was a poised and confident individual. He spoke with a booming, baritone voice that barely needed amplification, even to reach the extremes of the auditorium. He was eloquent, well-educated and naturally commanded respect.

On the other hand, Fred Lemon, reformed burglar of high renown, formerly in long-term residence at Her Majesty's pleasure was a nervous, reticent guy. He wriggled uncomfortably under the stage lights and when he spoke, the phrase 'Cockney Sparrow' sprang immediately to mind.

The most obvious feature of the evening, though, was not to do with the differences between these two men – actually, it was what they shared in common. You could tell, even from a distance, that despite the very many social, physical and historical inconsistencies that defined this unlikely duo there was, nevertheless, something very strong that bound them together. As they were interviewed, each man spoke of how Jesus Christ was in control of his life, but, even without the words, everyone could see for themselves the reality of that true, brotherly love that can bridge humanity's broadest social gulfs.

As a result of the testimonies of these two brothers in Christ, a number of unchurched people came to Christ that very evening, and others were significantly moved a stage or two closer on their own journey. What a brilliant picture of the grace and power of God at work – an ex-con and a top cop in partnership to change the world, one life at a time.

The evening had a powerful effect on me that has stayed with me ever since. It was a clear illustration of the spiritual truth of our oneness in the body of Christ: there is neither Jew nor

Greek, cop nor robber; all are one in Christ! And, in the years that followed, Debra and I became friends with a number of Christian police officers, including Robin Oake, who moved to the Isle of Man to become chief constable, ultimately retiring there a few years ago. Robin's son, Steve, was a member of our church during my training years and led a Bible study group for young teens. He followed his father into the police and eventually became a Special Branch officer. He was one of the first people we talked to in 1997 when God spoke to us about featuring the police as the main focus of one of our quarterly prayer gatherings. We had absolutely no idea that this would be the first step in a journey of fruitful partnership between police and churches.

Prayer support

Praying for the police was not something we'd ever thought about or heard about, but, as we sought the Lord's guidance in our core group meeting one day, we sensed that this was God's plan.

At the time, the police were suffering from an acute case of negative public relations. They have never been the most popular group of people in the land, even in the best of times, but things were worse than ever in the 1990s, with accusations of corruption, violence and poor management.

There was a perceived reduction of police presence on our streets; recruitment was a problem, especially among black and Asian people, and crime statistics were rising. The phrase 'law and order' became a political weapon employed by all the mainstream parties, and, as race riots exploded in different parts of the country, the extreme nationalist parties also entered the picture.

Probably the lowest point for police morale came as the preliminary findings of the Macpherson Report began to be leaked to the press and the phrase 'institutional racism' was coined to diagnose a condition from which the Metropolitan Police was apparently suffering. The report into the murder of a black teenager, Stephen Lawrence, at the hands of a gang of white youths in Eltham, south-east London, was not due for publication until 1999, but the public inquiry that informed the report was about to commence and, anyway, the media had been featuring the story regularly since the stabbing took place in April 1993. It wasn't the murder itself that fuelled the anger against the police but the way it had been investigated and, in particular, the different treatment that was allegedly received by black witnesses and white suspects.

We didn't intend to take sides in this debate, nor in any other, for that matter. What we felt was important was that our police needed to be supported in their hugely demanding task.

It seemed unjust that all that was ever said publicly about the police was negative and critical. Not that they shouldn't be criticised where this was due, but they also needed to be appreciated and encouraged for all the good that they did. Accountability is necessary in any organisation, especially in public services, but no group of people is perfect and everyone deserves praise and affirmation for their efforts and achievements. Approval and encouragement always seem to achieve more than mere fault-finding, as any parent or schoolteacher will verify. Surely God is pleased with the overall performance of the police and the relative balance of law and order we enjoy in our country.

Thank God for the police

Step one in our plan was to produce a quantity of posters, get them laminated for longevity and take them to police stations all over Greater Manchester to be displayed on their internal noticeboards.

We took a few minutes at the end of our next prayer event to explain the idea and to ask people to volunteer to do this in their own locality. There was a big response, and we were confident that, over the next few weeks, many of these posters would be prominently displayed in local 'nicks'.

Lee Hardy, then the youth pastor at Elmwood Church in Salford, recalls entering the doors of his local police station with a feeling of trepidation: 'I walked in with my knees knocking, feeling like I'd done something wrong and the sergeant glared at me, asking what I wanted. I explained in a squeaky voice that I was a Christian and that our church and others all over Manchester were praying especially for the police, and that we were holding a big prayer meeting in a couple of months' time. His countenance softened immediately. He took the poster and put it up there and then, thanking me and saying he appreci-ated it – even though he was not a believer himself. I came away delighted and felt sure God was going to do something special through this event.'

Here's what the poster said:

We would like to say a big

THANK YOU

To all police officers and civilian employees of
Greater Manchester Police.

Thank you for serving our society with commitment, diligence and integrity. Thank you for affording protection to the vulnerable, and for your efforts to maintain law and order for the benefit of all people in our region.

We are praying for you:

- That God would be with you in your work and in your leisure.

- That he would protect you and your families from evil.

- That you would know Christ's peace in your hearts and minds.

With love and appreciation on behalf of the whole Christian Community of Greater Manchester, from the core group of Prayer Network (an inter-church movement of prayer repre-senting thousands of Christians from most denominations) (*details of the meeting and contact telephone numbers*)

The evening itself was a big success. Around 800 packed into the King's Church building in the centre of Manchester on a cold January night. We interviewed and prayed for a number of different police officers, including big Steve Oake, who marched in rattling a pair of handcuffs while I was introducing the evening.

Grabbing the microphone off me, he addressed the gather-ing with some stern words about one of my previously undis-closed misdemeanours that, he said, had now come to light. He was taking me into custody to 'help with enquiries'. Even though I realised straight away that this was Debra's idea of a great set-up, I still experienced a momentary feeling of panic and was mightily relieved to see the cuffs disappear back into his pocket!

Steve shared about his life in the police force: how he was sure that God had called him to serve his kingdom through police work. At the time he was a driver in the traffic division, and he related how stressful and demanding this was, especially when accidents had to be attended. Often, the police arrive ahead of the ambulance and frequently find themselves having to deal with seriously injured victims. Even though they are well trained and in practice soon learn to deal professionally with traumatic circumstances, they are deeply affected by it all and many find unhealthy outlets for the tension that can build up.

He told us how vital his faith was in enabling him to deal properly with these sorts of pressures but also commented on how this attracted cynical and belittling attention from colleagues. Being a Christian in the police force, he said, was universally acknowledged as a sign of weakness: you were constantly ridiculed by fellow officers and always considered a fair target for humour, some of which went beyond the line of acceptability.

We stood to pray for Steve, and a few people came forward and laid hands on him. There was a strange moment when we'd finished and those praying returned to their places. Looking around, we could see no sign of our traffic cop. Debra whispered to me that he'd been bleeped in the middle of our prayer time and had left discreetly through a side door!

Other police officers we interviewed and prayed for on the night included Phil Gleave, Alison Fletcher, Neil Wain and Val Binstead, all of whom have been considerably used by God in their roles over these last few years. They each shared about the challenges and opportunities that faced them as Christians in the police; these ranged from the physical danger in which they often found themselves, to the occasional 'divine appointment' with a colleague or member of the public who would express interest in knowing God.

One common issue was the difficulty of balancing loyalty with honesty. One of the most important elements of serving in the police force is the total commitment needed between colleagues. Often this will demand discretion and confidentiality regarding personal information but sometimes this can involve being asked to cover for someone in a way that is not entirely transparent. The line between comradeship and integrity can be a fine and fragile one.

Church Christians

Also present on the night was a group of women that gave support to the wives of men who were in prison. We can't for the life of us recall how they came to be there, since not one of them was a Christian and their unease in the company of our other guests was clearly noticeable. Their stories, though, moistened the eyes of most of us as they talked about their voluntary work.

The leader of the group told us that she had only twice had any involvement with what she referred to as 'church Christians': one was negative, and one, happily for us, was positive. The first was when she had approached a local church to ask if they could hold a jumble sale to raise money for their cause. She was told that it would be all right as long as they referred to charity work in general rather than mentioned that the money would be used to help the families of criminals. Needless to say, the group managed to find an alternative venue for their jumble sale.

140

Fortunately, they had recently been offered a rent-free office in another church building, so they felt that things were all square again! They had numerous prayer requests and seemed happy enough to stand at the front surrounded by 'church Christians', hands raised in the prayer-hover position.

Like Steve, these ladies disappeared before the end of the evening, albeit for different reasons. We never heard from them after the event but hope they will count the evening as another positive experience. We certainly enjoyed their presence and were privileged to pray for them. Thankfully, the Lord is able to keep track of people and we trust that he'll use our brief encounter as a small part of the jigsaw of their lives.

Law and order

As well as the 7,000 police officers and the 3,000 support staff that made up Greater Manchester Police, we also prayed for other aspects of law enforcement, including the justice system, probation officers, prison officers, prison visitors, special constables and, yes, even traffic wardens!

It was interesting to hear from groups like: NACRO (National Association for the Care and Resettlement of Offenders), which was working to care for and help resettle those coming out of prison after serving a sentence; Victim Support – a group that helped those on the receiving end of crime to come to terms with the emotional, social and financial aspects of their circumstances and helped put people in touch with specialised support agencies where necessary; and, of course, the CPA – the interdenominational Christian Police Association that was founded over 100 years ago and now has branches in almost every force in the UK – which aims to promote and foster fellowship for Christian police officers, to demonstrate a relationship with God through a concern for righteousness on and

141

off duty, and to share the gospel with others, primarily within the police service. It's always encouraging to realise that God has his representatives in every sphere of society, and that he is working in an integrated way to advance his kingdom in our world.

Specific answers

It would be good if we were able to draw straight lines between the prayers we pray and the answers we see but often things are less clear, and there are many elements involved in the way God enables things to happen. We also need to be very careful to give God the glory for all he does, and not to imply in any way that answers he grants to prayers we pray are somehow to our credit. That said, though, we are very aware in Manchester of what seems to be a giant stride forward in the relationship between the police and the church during the last few years. And, as we'll see a little later, we have prayed specifically for crime reduction in our city and we have seen clear evidence of that happening in certain areas. Praise God!

One obvious example of an answer to prayer is the relationship between the police and The Message, which began in 1998, just a few months after this prayer event. The police had been running an annual summer campaign aimed at getting young people to channel their energies into activities that would benefit their communities. They called this Make a Difference, and each year tried to get youth groups and youngsters in general to co-operate in things like cleaning up a park, removing graffiti and so on.

By their own admission, the police were failing to inspire anything of real substance, despite the fact that they had a realistic budget and enthusiastic officers. Somehow, perhaps through contacts that were first made at the prayer evening, the two officers in charge of Make a Difference discovered that plans were underway for SSM2K. They'd heard that thousands of young people were coming to Manchester to celebrate the millennium in a Jesus-centred way by reaching out to the communities of Manchester in partnership with local churches. Each afternoon they would be travelling by coach to pre-arranged locations where they would get stuck in to exactly the kinds of projects that the police had been promoting.

These officers, Bob Collier and Phil Gleave, contacted Andy Hawthorne and asked for a meeting. The outcome was that Greater Manchester Police became one of the official sponsors of the mission, its logo and the Make a Difference banner appearing on the official publicity alongside those of Soul Survivor and The Message.

The police contributed significant funds from their crime reduction budget directly into the mission pot, and a number of officers played a full part in working with the teams in the community action sessions.

My abiding memory of the SSM2K mission sums up perfectly the truly amazing nature of this alliance between police and church. It was the final evening of the second week, the last night of the whole mission and the *Manchester Evening News* Arena was a heaving mass of humanity. We'd sung our praise songs and listened to inspirational preaching and the event was coming to a God-glorifying conclusion. PC Bob Collier, a man who had begun the fortnight referring to the thousands of Christians in tent-city as 'them' and by the midway point was using the pronoun 'we', stepped up to the microphone.

He'd been monitoring the crime statistics for one of our target areas, Swinton Valley, a notoriously tough place with a long list of daily incidents throughout the year, rising to its peak in the summer months. Each day for ten days, a thousand young

Christians had swarmed onto the estate and smiled their way through gruelling hard labour in gardens and wastelands. The visible end result was a physical transformation that the locals said they never dreamed possible.

There was, though, another feature of even more telling proportions, something that took us all by surprise. The daily invasion of the army of God had not only freshened the spiritual atmosphere and enhanced the physical landscape; it had also left an indelible mark on the record books.

'Question ...' Bob began, pacing the huge platform like a seasoned entertainer, 'How do you reduce the incidence of crime on one of Britain's toughest estates to zero for a ten-day period?' The dramatic pause was timed to perfection, and the vast auditorium fell silent in anticipation. 'Answer ... bring in the Christians!'

The noise was deafening as over 10,000 rose to their feet to cheer and applaud. Hallelujah! God was on the move! Not one crime had been committed on the Swinton Valley Estate during the whole mission: a statistic that was so unlikely it made the BBC website and has been quoted widely ever since.

This relationship has continued and developed since then, and similar joint ventures between the church and the police happened in 2001 as part of 2K1 in Salford, and again as part of Festival Manchester in 2002.

There's something very exciting about partnerships like these. When you see huge Christian banners bearing the official police shield like a stamp of approval, you can't help but lift your voice in praise of God. And when you hear that a senior police chief, in addressing a group of high-ranking officers on the subject of crime reduction, singled out prayer as the most effective tool, it does cause you to gasp in amazement!

When you think about it, the church and the police do have something in common in terms of their aims and objectives. The police exist not only to combat crime and catch criminals, but also to influence people positively towards observing the law willingly in order to provide a safer and happier community for everyone.

Like the church, they want to see society transformed not only in terms of lower crime statistics but also by steering young people away from the influences of negative role models and towards a way of life that makes a healthy contribution to society. Add to this the fact that many police officers are committed Christians and it's not difficult to imagine a future in which partnerships like this flourish all over the UK.

At a conference in London in 2001, for example, the Metropolitan Police Commissioner, Sir John Stevens, who describes himself as 'a committed but imperfect Christian', addressed the audience on the subject of tackling crime in the inner city. Referring to violence, drug abuse and gang membership he said, 'This is the darkness from which we have to pray for deliverance.' Bob Pull, who led the Christian Police Association at that time, said, 'Prayer can have an absolutely fundamental role in creating a peaceful community.'

If Christians will get serious about praying for the police as well as against crime, God will open doors for all kinds of exciting co-operative ventures, many of which may even qualify for funding from local crime reduction budgets.

Stephen Oake

Having referred to our late friend, Steve, in this chapter, it's only fitting to conclude with a tribute to him.

Steve was fatally stabbed during an anti-terrorist raid on a house in Manchester in January 2003. He was forty, married to

145

Lesley, and the father of three young children. He was praised for his bravery by the Prime Minister and the Chief Constable of GMP. His death had a profound effect on his colleagues, all of whom held him in high regard.

His Christian faith was well known to everyone, and a senior officer who worked closely with Steve said, 'He used to take a lot of stick for following Jesus, but, through the years he won many people over by his consistently Christlike way of life.' He went on to add, 'It used to be considered a weakness to be a Christian in the police. Now, in the light of Steve's long-term witness and now his tragic but heroic death, the whole thing has been turned on its head. Steve showed that it takes guts to be a disciple of Christ and a good number of his colleagues are now seriously seeking God for themselves through Alpha courses that are running in local police stations.'

eight
city linking

Debra

Inter-city unity

I think the idea of British cities 'twinning' with cities in other European countries first started in the 1970s. It was probably dreamt up by a bored local government officer in a chilly town hall somewhere in Yorkshire, inspired by the prospect of twice-yearly trips to a more picturesque and temperate place of work! Soon, just about every signboard that welcomed you to wherever also carried the name of its official French or German counterpart.

How valuable the exercise has been is difficult to measure – do you know, for example, if your town or city has a twin? I had to look on the Internet to discover that Manchester has three: Cordoba in Spain, Chemnitz in Germany and St Petersburg in Russia!

But whether the outcome of twinning is especially substantial or not, it's at least a step in the right direction. Anything that draws people together in any way at all is moving in the direction of the kingdom of God. There's so much rivalry and animosity in our world that any attempt to forge links between different groups of people is surely something that pleases God.

This is another principle we stumbled across as we sought to follow God's leading: that God's agenda not only includes unity within a city but also between cities. It would be great to be able to say that we sat down and worked this out for ourselves, or that God spoke powerfully to us during a prayer time, but in actual fact neither could be further from the truth.

We discovered it as a result of inviting Ed Silvoso to come and speak at a conference we were organising in the late 1990s. His insights into the whole area of city-reaching had impacted us greatly, and we wanted to make them known as widely as possible within Manchester.

Ed's book, *That None Should Perish*, was a huge seller, and his ministry at that time was very much appreciated across Europe.

Incidentally, Frank and I were part of the team at Spring Harvest in the early 1990s when Ed first came to the attention of the British Christian public. He'd been invited as a seminar speaker and faithfully shared his thoughts from marquee to marquee around the Skegness site to groups of 100 or so. After the first day, his seminars were attracting such huge crowds that the site leadership team had to switch them to the Big Top!

His teaching was so clearly from the heart of God and so powerfully communicated that he was asked to stay for the rest of Spring Harvest, and was eventually shuttled between the sites like the VIP he truly is.

His passion is to see Christians of different groupings co-operating in evangelism but he argues strongly that no such activity ought to begin until those groupings learn to pray together. This demands repentance of former attitudes and of

148

isolated strategies and a determined and dedicated approach to building relationships of mutual respect and affirmation, all of which we'd been working away at for years in Manchester.

Twinning our cities for God

Ed challenged us to broaden our horizons and not only organise a conference for Manchester but to twin with our nearest city and make it a joint event. Not only would such a venture be a bigger and more inspiring occasion but it would also be a powerful symbol of unity in the body of Christ and of the values of the kingdom of God. In fact, he insisted that we do it, saying that if we didn't he wouldn't come!

So, in faith, we agreed. We would host a Cities For God conference in partnership with Liverpool, a city we knew nothing about and in which we had no Christian contacts at all!

The core group sat down and started to brainstorm. Surely one of us must know somebody in Liverpool. Fortunately, one of us did. Michael Harvey had a friend, John Cavanagh, who'd moved from Manchester many years ago and was involved in a church somewhere on the outskirts of Liverpool. He would contact him and see if he could put us in touch with any of the movers and shakers in the region.

Amazingly, it turned out that John was closely involved in a very recently formed group of church leaders from the whole of the Merseyside area, known as Together For the Harvest (TFH), along with Nic Harding, who leads Frontline Church in Liverpool. TFH's vision was (and still is) to network as many churches together as possible, so that every man, woman and child in Merseyside is repeatedly presented with the gospel.

Michael arranged for us all to meet to discuss the idea of a joint conference and, within a few days, we found ourselves chatting away like long-lost friends. Isn't it great how God brings

149

people together? We'd never met these people before and yet we clicked instantly, not just because we shared common values and goals but also at the ordinary human level – we liked each other!

Joking apart

It turned out that Nic and John were two key actors in terms of churches working together in Liverpool, and so it wasn't long before we'd put together a working group and got the ball rolling for our conference.

It was in our planning meetings that we first spotted the depth of division that seemed to exist between our two cities. There was a lot of good-natured banter between the two 'sides', pointing out the perceived strengths and weaknesses between the two cities, but underneath it all we could sense that we were tapping into some fairly unhealthy spiritual strongholds.

For example, even though John had lived on Merseyside for most of his life, he still clung proudly to his Mancunian roots, often referring to himself as 'living in exile' or as a 'missionary to the heathen Scousers'!

Oasis, the Manchester-based rock band, were flying high in the charts at the time yet they were frequently dismissed by one member of the Liverpool group as 'the poor man's Beatles'!

Without thinking, Frank would mimic the Liverpool accent from time to time in a stereotypically derogatory way, not really thinking about whether or not people might feel offended.

Since we were all working together on the same project, we happily accepted all this banter as just a bit of fun, but the more Frank and I reflected on it, the more aware we became of the reality of the strength of feelings that existed between the two cities. We knew we were actually feeding the issue by tapping into these spiritual roots, and we made a conscious decision to stop.

It wasn't only true at the popular level – people poking fun about football, fashion and accents – it was also prevalent in economic and governmental circles. For example, around that time plans were being proposed for a second runway at Manchester Airport. Liverpool City Council was strongly opposed to these plans, on the grounds that its own airport ought to be developed instead. Manchester already enjoyed a high level of air traffic, which brought much prosperity to the region. Another runway would not only increase that but also push Liverpool further down the scale.

As we followed the debate in the press and on TV, we saw that not only was there intense commercial rivalry between the two cities, but there were also issues of pride and reputation underlying the points being made.

We'd never really thought about it before, but the more we worked together in this inter-city planning group the greater our sense became of a real antipathy between Manchester and Liverpool – something far greater than just the knockabout jocularity between Scousers and Mancs, maybe something along the lines of the spiritual principalities and powers referred to in the New Testament. We decided that we needed to address this at the conference.

Two into one

The venue was King's Park Christian Centre in Leigh, a large town situated halfway between Liverpool and Manchester. It had a 1,000-seater auditorium that was soon buzzing with that tell-tale sound of people feeling comfortable with each other.

I always enjoy the atmosphere at the start of a big inter-church gathering when people are taking their seats alongside people they've never met before and yet immediately feel at home with. There are no questions about denominational allegiance, no references made to doctrinal differences and so on, just a sense of family, a warmth of belonging that gives a hint of eternal destiny.

We welcomed everyone, sang some worship songs together and introduced Ed Silvoso. Ed took to the stage with his Bible in one hand and a cup of tea balanced on a saucer in the other. Everyone was intrigued as he talked and sipped his way through the first session, asking, at halfway point, for a top-up!

Drawing largely on Paul's letter to the Ephesians, he laid out his first principles in great detail: that unity between Christians is the foundation of effective city-reaching mission. And that the first step of unity must be taken on our knees.

We had a break and then we gave the whole of the next session over to praying for unity between our two cities.

First of all, we asked all the leaders to come forward and stand on either side of the platform: Liverpool on the left; Manchester on the right. Then we spoke for a few minutes about the sense of hostility there seemed to be between the two cities, explaining how we interpreted this as something in the spiritual realm, not just a matter of human attitudes or activity.

One by one, each leader said a few words, mostly confessing something fairly minor but acknowledging that it did indeed represent a spirit of competition or pride. Frank was visibly moved as he confessed having sung profane and antagonistic football chants directed at Liverpool and Everton fans as a teenager. It had seemed amusing at the time, he explained, but now caused him to feel deeply ashamed.

As the repentance flowed, so too did the tears. One by one, people began to embrace all around the auditorium, starting with those on the platform and spreading rapidly through the entire gathering. Whatever deep-seated divides had been brought into the conference were quickly bridged as Mancunians and Merseysiders sought each other out and hugged, wept and prayed together. It was a truly wonderful moment.

The sense of the presence of God was powerfully discernible. And the praying kept going as people moved spontaneously around to find a member of the 'other side' and to ask and grant forgiveness and grace.

Eventually, we drew things to a close with some formal prayers from the front followed by an exchange of gifts in typical city-twinning style. For some reason, Michael Harvey had brought a large, yellow soft toy in the shape of a bee! Despite the fact that none of us had ever heard about it, he was adamant that the worker bee is the official symbol of Manchester: the industrious city. Frank says it probably has more to do with Michael's own personal interest in Boddington's, the well-known Manchester brewery that features a bee in its logo!

Representing Merseyside, John Cavanagh's contribution was a Liverpool FC pennant, which Michael, a staunch Manchester United fan, had great difficulty in accepting graciously!

Finally, everyone stood and joined hands as Ed led us in prayer, asking God to bless our unity and to use it for his glory, not only as an effective tool for mission but also as a beacon to the rest of the nation. Then he picked up his cup and saucer and carried on teaching!

It was a remarkable conference that will remain in the memory of everyone who attended. We believe God did something special between the two cities that day, something that began to reverse the trend of separation and enmity. Since then, there has been evidence of increased co-operation not only between Christian groups but also in business and civic circles.

For example, in 2001, the leaders of Manchester and Liverpool city councils met together in Manchester's Bridgewater Hall and signed a formal agreement to co-operate together wherever possible for the benefit of the whole region. The statement, entitled 'Liverpool/Manchester Joint City Concordat', represented a major breakthrough in the relationship between the two cities that had previously been marked entirely by competitive attitudes at every level of business, finance and cultural services, tourism, transport, higher education and regeneration. The meeting was attended by the Deputy Prime Minister John Prescott, who said, 'Liverpool and Manchester have so much in common and so much to learn from one another.'

On the Christian scene, Manchester and Liverpool have helped and inspired each other in a number of ways. For example, during our preparations for Festival Manchester, some church leaders from Liverpool began to sense God calling them to hold a similar mission.

They attended a number of our planning meetings to learn in advance how the whole thing worked, and they also challenged their own people to pray for us. Hundreds of delegates came from Merseyside to take part in Festival Manchester as a result of these relationships of mutual support and encouragement. Also, a number of key intercessors joined our prayer teams for the same event.

We're planning to support them as much as possible during Merseyfest, their version of Festival Manchester, which was in the advanced stages of planning while we were writing this. How good and pleasant it is when brothers and sisters dwell together in unity.

Revival road?

Some time after our landmark conference, I came across a prophetic word in a book by Graham Cooke that made me tremble as I read it. Written a good few years before, it speaks, at one point, of God's heart for unity in our land and foretold of conferences and conventions where cities would express repentance and forgiveness – even specifying Manchester and Liverpool by name! Imagine how encouraged I felt as I read this:

> Unity is the great target of the Holy Spirit in the 1990s and beyond. We will see a move of God occur that will cut across all streams. The day of the streams is over; the day of the river has begun. There will be a United Kingdom. I used to think the name was a joke. However in 1983 the Lord showed me it was a prophetic name. The Lord is raising up champions who will have a tremendous anointing for unity, who will turn the hearts of the nations towards each other. Lack of unity is a major stranglehold on revival. We will have conferences and conventions, not just aimed at speaking for unity but actively promoting reconciliation, apology and restoration. Forgiveness and healing will flow. The North/South divide in England will perish. Inter-county and inter-city rivalry will die. Lancashire will stop fighting the War of the Roses with York-shire. Cities will be twinned in heart and spirit. Liverpool will stop hating Manchester. This kind of rivalry is repeated throughout the nation. In the realm of the Spirit, England must recognise that she needs her Celtic brothers. Repentance must flow; ancient hatreds must be laid down. These conferences will be devoted to tearing down strongholds of history, bigotry, treachery and betrayal. As

these things are finally dealt with, we will see economic and spiritual revival breaking out in these areas.

Graham Cooke's prophecy in *Developing your Prophetic Gifting* published by Sovereign World in 1994.

There's clearly a long way to go before the rest of this prophecy comes to fulfilment, but praise God for the green shoots we can already see!

what's the secret?

Frank

Will anybody come this time?

We were enjoying the unusual experience of driving against the rush-hour traffic. The heavy rain compounded the homeward crawl for the thousands of commuters on the opposite carriage-way as we breezed along into town on the evening of another big prayer gathering.

On the back seat were thousands of flyers to be put out on seats, a dozen plastic buckets for the offering, copies of the evening's running order and a huge rolled-up banner we'd had specially made for the evening. The publicity had been out for weeks; the date had been put in diaries months ago; all the planning was done, and all that was needed now was the last-minute checks on the venue, briefing of stewards and our usual half-hour of prayer with the core group and musicians.

I only realised that Debra had been anticipating my predict-able comment once the first couple of words were out of my mouth. In her annoyingly astute way, she was finishing off my statement for me, speaking out the very words that were still travelling from my brain to my tongue. 'I don't think there'll be many turning up tonight ...' I said, my words trailing off in embarrassment as I heard them in stereo. Rallying quickly, I began to point out the reasons for what she calls my pessimism but I refer to as realism.

First of all, it was a wet and windy winter Wednesday. Secondly, at precisely the same time as our event was due to start, Manchester United would be kicking off in an important home game that was also being shown live on terrestrial TV. Thirdly, for those who didn't like football, there was *Corrie*. And tonight's special episode had been advertised for weeks by Granada. Who would want to fight the elements and traipse into town for a prayer meeting after a hard day at work when they could put their feet up and be entertained in the comfort of their own lounge?

'Ever the pessimist!' Debra smiled. 'We'll see,' I murmured, recalling the many times I'd made the same erroneous prediction at more or less the same point on the journey! I guess it was my way of preparing for the worst. Thankfully, I have managed to change since those days – probably given the evidence of dozens of packed houses on similar subsequent nights.

Numbers game?

But does it matter whether people turn out in large numbers? Aren't our prayers effective even when only two or three are gathered together? From the earliest days of Prayer Network, we were very aware of the 'quantity versus quality' debate, the prevailing wisdom being that the success of a prayer meeting is not dependent on the number of people present but on their faith and their capacity to pray in line with the will of God as led by the Holy Spirit.

Of course, this is true (actually it's a truism), but how on earth can it not be better to have hundreds of people praying for a city rather than just a few? I remember a preacher once contradicting the popular myth that numbers don't matter to God with the comment, 'Of course numbers matter to God – he named a whole book after them!'

Not everyone agrees with this view, though. We've been accused of empire-building in some quarters, and even anathematised by one national prayer group on the grounds that we resort to worldly methods to draw a crowd. Apparently, any prayer event that attracts large numbers must *per se* be something not inspired or blessed by God! I think such thinking reflects a twisted logic born out of a 'remnantitis' theology. Some Christians have been taught to believe that the world is bad and getting worse and therefore they should huddle together in small groups waiting for Jesus to return and resisting the pressure to conform to anything that smacks of success. Church should be dull; Christians should never enjoy anything, and any attempt to present the gospel to the outside world must be offensive. Prayer meetings, by definition, are meant to be small and boring and attended by senior citizens with beards, some of whom are male.

Our theology differs greatly from this. We believe that the kingdom of God is advancing on the earth and, like the yeast in the dough that Jesus spoke about in one of his parables (Matthew 13:33), our task is to permeate the world and bring change that glorifies the King.

We believe that our faith should sit at the centre of our lives and provide a basis for the celebration and enjoyment of creation, which is marred by sin but still intrinsically good. The global church is growing in size and significance and we should be going about Father's business joyfully and visibly.

From the start of Prayer Network, our goal was to get as many people to pray for the city as possible. Not just attending the events but actually praying: praying on the night; taking home prayer requests to share in small groups; taking home prayer issues to the local church; praying for the city. And we believe that prayer can and should be enjoyable, not necessarily onerous. Of course, there are times when prayer is hard work but that needn't imply that all prayer is a struggle.

It's such a shame that some Christians seem to be completely negative about the outworking of their faith. The fact that large numbers do turn out to pray and continually feed back how much they enjoy the occasion has always suggested to us that we're on the right tracks. It encourages us to know that literally thousands of Christians are enjoying praying for their city. We're absolutely convinced that God is involved, and that he is pleased that the prayer burden is being shared so widely.

Special recipe?

Because of these consistently high turnouts, one of the most frequently asked questions we get is to do with an analysis of the model we've used: What's the secret – is there a formula?

As you'd expect, we always respond by pointing out that God is the prime mover. We're simply following the leading of the Holy Spirit, and seem to be tapping into his heart for unified prayer. God must receive the glory for any aspect of our work that pleases him and blesses the city.

But we're not of the opinion that God operates people like puppets, overruling personality, intellect and skills. On the contrary, it seems clear from the Bible that God gives gifts to his people, expecting them to be used to serve the purposes of his kingdom.

God calls us his co-workers, and delights to work with us and through us. His Spirit energises and directs us as we use our God-given faculties. This seems especially true when we work together in groups that reflect a breadth of Christian experience and churchmanship.

With this in mind, then, Debra and I have reflected on and analysed the way the prayer movement in Manchester developed over the years, and we'd like to offer what we consider to be the key elements of our particular approach.

It may be that you feel called to start a similar prayer movement in your locality; if so, these principles and values may provide you with some useful ideas. The following points are not being put forward as a formula, or even as guidelines. They are, however, crucial factors in our model of stimulating and enabling city-wide, cross-church prayer.

Ownership

One of our earliest, conscious goals was to make sure that we had the widest possible support from churches, especially those that were growing and full of life. Unfortunately, some of these didn't have a great track record of co-operating across different denominations or streams.

We understood that the reasons for this were many, some to do with theological differences, others simply because of the sheer busy-ness and sharp, distinctive focus of the churches themselves.

Many churches were also very actively involved within their own national or international groups, leaving little time or energy for yet another level of relating. But we couldn't shake off the sense that God was calling the church in Manchester to a new level of unity and co-operation for the kingdom, and we

161

were determined to get representatives from a healthy cross-section to form our organising group.

Amazingly, our timing could not have been better. Just when it looked like we would need a miracle to remove the barriers of suspicion and fear that tend to separate church leaders in cities like ours, God decided to pour out his Spirit in an astonishing way in what came to be known as the Toronto Blessing. There was a particular window of about a year during which Debra and I would frequently find ourselves in surprising settings with the Holy Spirit turning up in power.

On one occasion, we were embroiled in a tense discussion with some church leaders who were very concerned about structural issues. They had differing ideas about how inter-church groups should be governed, and we couldn't seem to agree on how large prayer meetings ought to be run.

After about an hour of polite but fruitless discussion, some-one said, 'Let's pray together.' Fifteen minutes later, we were all laughing uncontrollably as the Holy Spirit came upon us and smudged all our strongly held opinions! I can still picture one guy, a short and somewhat portly figure, literally rolling from side to side on the floor like a giant Easter egg with arms and legs! Once we'd managed to compose ourselves and return to our agenda, everything seemed a lot less controversial and we soon found compromises and solutions.

Using different venues for the prayer gatherings was one factor that helped gain ownership. We're all creatures of habit, and many people seem more willing to come to an inter-church prayer evening when it's in their building! Once they experience for themselves the blessing of praying with others, enjoying new styles of worship and finding out about all kinds of new and exciting ministries that are happening across their city, they're usually (though not always) happy to do it again next time, even though it may well mean crossing the threshold of a strange building in another part of town.

Getting church leaders on board was another key ingredient. Debra continued to knock on doors and 'sell' the vision to dozens of leaders of different churches and ministries. One or two were decidedly frosty but most warmed to her non-threatening personality and appreciated the vision. The majority agreed at least to publicise our events.

A common occurrence was that some leaders, on hearing the word 'prayer', automatically went into default-and-delegate mode. Knowing there were a few people in their church who were prayer enthusiasts, they would assume that our goal was to network the intercessors.

Debra tells the story of a telephone conversation she had with David Hughes, the Rector of Emmanuel and St James in Didsbury, just up the road from us in south Manchester. She'd rung to ask if he could include an announcement in their church bulletin about the next prayer event, and he'd promised to alert the 'prayer warriors'. She asked him whether or not he believed that all Christians needed to pray and he went silent for a moment. 'Yes,' he responded eventually; then there was a pause, followed by: 'You're absolutely right! Why don't you come and speak about that on Sunday?' He has since become a valuable colleague in the prayer movement, as well as a very good friend.

Excellence

Doing things well is, sadly, another of our values that attracts criticism. This is probably one of those 'worldly methods' that cause offence in some circles. The argument seems to suggest that if things are well organised and well presented, then perhaps too much 'flesh' and not enough 'Spirit' has been used.

Professionalism is the common censure: as though slapdash amateurism was some kind of spiritual virtue.

Some Christians seem to have grown accustomed to events that have been poorly planned, not publicised in time, under-funded, allowed to start and finish late and led by a verbose pensioner with the charisma of a tailor's dummy. Anything that deviates too much from the familiar makes them uncomfortable and therefore can't be right!

As well as bathing our ideas in prayer, we set out from the start to do everything humanly possible to plan and present our events excellently. This is not just because we believe this glorifies God but also because it honours and blesses the people who turn up and take part.

We ask the different worship groups we invite to rehearse their songs together well before the event and to arrive early for sound checks. We hire professional PA and video equipment and pay for experienced technical operators. We produce high-quality posters and leaflets to promote our events and distribute them widely well ahead of time. We use the Internet, email and text messaging as well as snail mail to keep the date in front of people as it draws near.

All this is time-consuming and demanding work, and costly in terms of finances. However, it is more effective than 'just trusting the Lord', when that is an excuse to sit back and do nothing. And our offerings on the night always cover the costs.

We've been so blessed by the skills and commitment of a few really gifted people over the years. Of special mention is our friend Paul Keeble, who is not only a technical genius but also a very competent writer, graphic artist and ideas man. Paul was one of the founder members of Prayer Network, without whom our publicity and PA would never have been so consistently superb. He and his wife, Judith, are missionaries to urban

Manchester, having moved from the comfort of a suburban upbringing into a demanding and dangerous inner-city area many years ago. From day one, Paul played a vital role in the core group, and his own high standards have influenced the rest of us in many ways.

Another is Mike Chesterton, a Tear Fund executive we've known for 25 years. Mike enjoys co-ordinating the stewards for our events and looking after the offering: hugely important tasks but demanding a truly servant heart.

Packing a lot into an evening can be a dangerous thing to do without thinking carefully about how long each component will realistically take. We always put our running order together in advance of the evening, communicating clearly and firmly to every participant exactly how much (or rather, how little) time they can be allowed for their slot.

We work back from our target finish time, usually 9.45 pm from a 7.30 pm start, and assign each element of the pro-gramme an exact time. We build in a few buffers here and there to be realistic, but we keep them to ourselves. Often we'll deviate from the plan as the Spirit leads on the evening, but at least we know what we need to adjust as we go.

We never, ever run over. People hate being stuck in their seats while a meeting is allowed to meander aimlessly into the night by leaders who don't seem to have a life. Conversely, we've discovered that when a meeting finishes earlier than expected, people enjoy hanging on and chatting for ages (having fellowship is the technical term!). It's to do with being empowered and released instead of controlled and patronised.

Inclusivity

After our first few meetings, we came to the conclusion that inviting a guest speaker was not what we should be doing. It sent out the wrong signals about what the evening was about, suggesting that it was more akin to a traditional 'celebration' with a bit of prayer tacked on, when we were determined that prayer should be the central activity.

Furthermore, we realised that certain speakers would attract some people but not others; that's just a fact of life and another challenge to unity. So, 'no more big names' became one of our values. And the other side of that is that everyone who attends is expected to play her or his part. Recognising that every tradition has a different idea of how to pray, we agreed that affirming every style of prayer would be a discipline we would always follow.

This was a real challenge to some of us, especially the more demonstrative and expressive members of the core group who may secretly have felt that noisy and dramatic prayer is actually more effective than the quiet, reflective sort! In practice, it became a real challenge to everyone when we would ask people to get into small groups with people they didn't know. There were some very interesting facial expressions on display as the different traditions mixed together.

One particularly moving occasion occurred in Manchester Cathedral, when someone came forward and suggested that we kneel together and pray the Lord's Prayer. For some of the more overtly liberated ones, this was just as threatening as it was for the more liturgical to join in with the 'Korean style', all-out-loud-at-once prayers that we often included in the pro-gramme. But everyone knelt and a hush fell on the gathering.

I began to lead and the sense of God's presence was immediate and awesome. How pleased he must have been that hundreds of people from across the denominational spectrum were humbling themselves for the sake of the city. His presence was so heavy that we remained in silence for a minute or two

166

after the amen. It evoked a sense of the outpoured blessing of God spoken of in Psalm 133: good, pleasant, fragrant and commanded by God in response to the unity of his people.

Connectivity

We always work hard to communicate relevantly with the people who attend the prayer evenings. Both style and substance are important to us as we seek to be informative and challenging. Our meetings follow a fast-moving magazine format with a TV feel: short, snappy interviews interspersed with creative prayer slots in groups of different sizes.

Thinking back, this is a model I first came across about twenty years ago under the title of Prayer Concerts: events aimed at Christian teenagers organised by Youth For Christ. If I remember correctly, the idea was pioneered by Trevor Gregory, a YFC Centre Director in Hull, and Jon Earwicker from their national leadership team helped to bring the model to a wider audience through Spring Harvest.

The concept was based on the fact that most young people have a short attention span, making traditional prayer meetings particularly uninviting for them. Breaking the evening down into bite-sized chunks makes it more accessible. And the truth is that all ages appreciate the faster pace. Like it or not, we've been conditioned by the media to expect and respond to small, intensive bursts of information and activity. Then, when we need a bit more time to deal with something, everyone still has some stamina left.

Helping people to know how to pray intelligently for specific issues is another way to enable effective prayer and keep people interested and involved. Rather than simply challenging people to 'pray for Manchester', we choose a specific theme, as explained in Chapter 4: important areas of life that affect all of us and that God is concerned about.

We research the subject over many weeks to find out what the key issues are and we always come across Christians working quietly away to see the kingdom of God come into that specific area of society. The information is published and given out on the night to all who attend. We've heard many times from people who are still using these fact sheets (Updates) many months later in their personal prayer times.

Whatever theme we follow, we always come across God's people working in some related service or group. We invite them to come, be interviewed and share their prayer needs. On the night, we'll pray for them and cry out to God for his power to increase through their efforts.

We frequently invite non-Christians who carry responsibility in the areas that we're focusing on to come and be prayed for too, and rarely does anyone turn us down. It was a real pleasure, for example, to interview a number of MPs and local councillors when we got together in election year to pray for those in authority. Many appeared visibly moved and genuinely appreciated our support.

Informality

Debra and I host our meetings in a deliberately light-hearted way. We often poke fun at ourselves to make people feel at home and to remove any idea that those at the front are in some way more special than those in the pews.

We also enjoy a bit of a laugh with the people who come to talk about their work or share their prayer points. We don't really work at this; it just comes naturally to both of us. We have different styles that work well together and we enjoy the challenge of live presenting. Someone once referred to us as the church's Richard and Judy, which we think was intended as a compliment!

It may seem a small point but, in fact, the way an evening like this is hosted is absolutely crucial. The people at the front really need to be relaxed and at ease with themselves to create an atmosphere where everyone feels comfortable and welcome. This is especially important when there is a breadth of different traditions present.

In addition, a great deal of sensitivity and tact are needed, as well as the ability to think on one's feet. Trying to make people laugh as an end in itself can cause offence, especially when 'in' humour is used or 'cheap shots' are taken at individuals or groups. Sometimes, what was meant to be funny can end up looking like a dig or a mickey-take.

In any case, informality is not the same as humour. The key to being informal is to be yourself and to cultivate a genuine determination not to take yourself too seriously.

We trace back our healthy disregard for excessive formality to a few key people who influenced us in the formative stages of our walk with God: people like Jeff Lucas, Roger Ellis and Gerald Coates (whose strong views on non-religious Christianity played a major role in shaping our theology and the way we live out our faith), all of whom demonstrate a fun approach to faith that we've always warmed to. Bryce Cooke, who for years presented a weekly Christian programme on one of Manchester's leading commercial radio stations, also taught me, as a young Christian working alongside him on air, to cultivate a non-religious approach, especially when conducting interviews on behalf of a broadcast audience.

We simply try to be real, stay focused on the task and the timing, remain aware of the variety of churchmanship and expectations, and put people at ease. The nice thing for us is that we enjoy it – at least we realise that we have done once the evening is over; we're usually too busy concentrating to enjoy the live programme while it's actually happening.

Positive perspective

One of our strongest distinctives in the way we go about praying for our city is that we always adopt an affirming stance rather than a critical one. It's easy to see what's wrong with society but laying into its shortcomings doesn't seem to achieve anything, even when couched in the technical jargon of so-called spiritual warfare.

Now, I realise that I'm making myself vulnerable to misunderstanding here, so I will explain what I'm saying and what I'm not.

There are groups for whom prayer and spiritual warfare begin with a negative analysis of society and then focus on certain aspects of that analysis by praying against things. Sometimes the things that are prayed against are assigned a cosmic significance by attaching to them the phrase 'spirit of'. For example, in a city in which homosexuality is rife, some Christians will pray against the 'spirit of homosexuality over the city'.

In the context of this book, I'm not going to get into a detailed discussion about this approach, neither am I suggesting that it's wrong. All I am saying is that our approach tends to be the opposite of this.

Our analysis of our city, while not unaware of the obvious problems that exist, deliberately focuses on those aspects that are good but in need of more support and encouragement.

Our hospitals, for example, creaking as they are under the sheer volume of patients' needs and lacking the funds and expertise they need to deliver the goods perfectly, are neverthe-less performing valiantly. Many of their employees work long hours for less pay than they deserve. Some are Christians, serving in a particular role and location because they are called by God to be there.

Rather than praying against particular political policies or denouncing any spirit of mismanagement, we would rather bless the amazing work that is being done and pray for the nursing staff, doctors, auxiliary workers, paramedics, adminis-trators and so on. We pray that God will bless them and empower them to carry on, especially in the face of discourage-ment and opposition.

Other prayer groups may focus on the past sins of the city and then move into times of repenting on behalf of them (Identificational Repentance). In our early days we were involved in this to a degree (for example, the Peterloo Massacre referred to in Chapter 1), but felt after a while that it had the potential to hold us in a retrospective and somewhat depress-ing mindset.

I have reflected theologically on this subject and have written papers for the Evangelical Alliance and others setting out my thoughts (I have included one in the appendix for those who wish to study the subject further). Our considered position nowadays is that God is calling us to pray for the present and future of our city. We have prayed about some elements of its past and feel, in our case, that the priority now is to move on.

We acknowledge the influence of a number of people who have contributed to our positive approach to praying for the city. In particular, Pieter Bos, a Dutch theologian and practitioner who taught us to seek what he called 'God's redemptive purpose' for the city. He urged us to identify what God had put into the heart of our city and then work with that to see it advance and expand.

We reckon that Manchester is a pioneering and industrious city as well being musical and artistic. This has helped us in considering how to pray along the lines of God's plans and purposes for the city. Stuart Murray's book, *God Loves the City,* helped shape our thoughts, as did the late Tom Marshall, whose book, *Principalities and Powers,* contains some insightful teaching on the nature and purpose of cities in God's plans.

In the early 1990s, we had the privilege of attending a series of Tom's seminars on the subject of winning cities, and were blessed and challenged in equal measure. He taught that the city has a persona of its own that can be shaped and influenced either for good or evil. When a city is struggling, it needs encouraging. Like a person who wants the best for their friend, we should speak to that which is good in the spirit of our city and encourage it to increase.

Robert Warren holds a similar view drawing on the references to 'the angel of the church' in the first three chapters of Revelation. The angel addressed here by the risen Jesus may refer to the spiritual expression of the particular church, its persona; the spiritual personification that came into being in the heavenly realm when the church was formed on the earth.

This spiritual reality can be addressed in a personal way that can affect its destiny. In the case of the seven churches referred to, most were commended and encouraged for something they were doing well, even if only a small thing ('you ... have not grown weary', 'you did not renounce your faith'). There is no hiding the failures of these churches but they are praised and affirmed wherever possible.

172

Taking a positive approach as we pray for our town or city is a way of thanking and praising God for the evidence of his goodness in the creation and the work of his Spirit through his people to date. If all we do is point out faults and failings, we're guilty of the opposite of worship, whatever that is! The apostle Paul encourages believers to focus their minds on things that are good and worthy of praise (Philippians 4:8). For many of us, this requires a deliberate determination, especially when we're bombarded hourly through the media with negative images of our world.

Figurehead

All the above values have played an important role in the effectiveness of Prayer Network but there is one contributing factor that, in my opinion, stands out above all the others. That is the key role of its founder and leader, Debra Green. Although I realise that my bias is clear, I believe that this is a general principle anyway; however, in Christian circles, it often remains unrecognised due to a faulty understanding of humility.

Let's be clear about this: when one person has an idea or a vision (whether it's spoken about in spiritual language or not), and they turn it into a tangible, fruitful reality by persuading others to join them and by sustaining huge effort over a long period of time, surely that person deserves credit.

Andy Hawthorne has a similar position in The Message. The amazing success of The Tribe and all their related ministries has been achieved by lots of people pooling their talents, time and energies under God and giving their lives away for the lost kids of Manchester. But, without Andy's passion, vision and total commitment at the centre of all of that, not much of it would ever have happened.

He lives and breathes his ministry, and his enthusiasm is infectious and creative: it causes people to rise up in faith and step out for God. Sure, he's part of a team, and he's the first to acknowledge the high quality of the people around him. But you ask any one of them where The Message would be today without Andy and they would all say the same: nowhere! God works through people, and he chooses his people wisely.

In reality, Debra doesn't need me to fight her corner any more, although I frequently had to in the early years when people would mistakenly refer to me as the founder and leader, probably because I'm a man and their limited experience of women didn't include any examples of effective leadership! There are literally thousands of Christians in Manchester and hundreds in other parts of the world that appreciate the central role she's playing in our city.

God called Debra to this ministry because he knows she has the gifts and personality to make it work. She cares passionately about unity, prayer and mission, and has a way of inspiring others to feel the same way. She's prophetic and yet gets along brilliantly with those in pastoral, evangelistic and apostolic roles. Her winsome manner makes it almost impossible for people not to warm to her (with one or two notable exceptions!), and her depth of understanding of church and great respect for its many expressions keep her in that Radical Middle Ground necessary for effective networking.

I'm saying all this not to get some Brownie points (although you can never have too many!) but to try to ensure that the vital role of a gifted leader/networker is not overlooked: someone called and equipped by God to serve as catalyst and exemplar; someone with the character, personality, credibility, motivation and energy to rise to the challenge and take others with them.

If no such person is immediately evident, perhaps the best thing to do is pray for God to raise someone up with the right set of personal qualities. There's no better way to prevent unity than sending the wrong person out to try and promote it!

Principles, values and guidelines alone can never enable a network of city-wide prayer. Anointed leadership is the most important element of all. I thank God for Debra and consider it a privilege to be a member of her team.

Special circumstances

The principles I have set out in this chapter are certainly transportable and following them will help establish a prayer movement in any town or city. But there are other elements that need to be borne in mind when reflecting on what God has done in Manchester over this past decade or so. There were a number of opportunities that opened up to us that can't be reproduced by any human effort, and we want to continue to remind ourselves of God's sovereign hand in all we have seen emerge.

The Toronto Blessing certainly helped a great deal to lower the barriers of caution between leaders. It's hard to retain a formal or uneasy 'distance' with someone while 'doing carpet time' together! No one can contrive a move of God that sweeps through churches and softens the hearts of leaders to one another.

The growing impact of The Tribe and the expanding work of The Message Trust, which delivers effective discipleship to youngsters in partnership with local churches, were major elements in shaping our ministry to the city. Not every city has an Andy Hawthorne figure or a high-profile band like The Tribe.

The fact that the Millennium was imminent undoubtedly affected the lives of many believers, in some cases creating a clearer sense of belonging to the wider body of Christ and a willingness to demonstrate that in quite unprecedented ways. Such moments of opportunity are extremely rare.

Unique as these factors are, however, their absence elsewhere ought not discourage others from rising to the challenge of organising city-changing prayer. I'm convinced that God is calling his church to unite and seek his face for the transformation of communities across the world, and each area will have its own unique set of circumstances. The opportunities for blessing will be limited only by the faith, energy, commitment, creativity and humility of his people. Imagine how different your town or city could be if its spiritual walls were rebuilt! Imagine what new and exciting ministries might be birthed within an environment of inter-church unity and fervent prayer!

ten
behold!... new things

Debra

Taking stock

During the last few years we've become aware of the need to renew and refresh things in order to maintain the momentum of prayer that has built up in our city.

It's easy to slip into complacency when large numbers of people are turning out regularly for special events: a new comfort zone comes into being that, in itself, can become a barrier to God's agenda to do more new things as he works through his people to transform society. The challenge has been to find new ways of developing and growing the prayer movement while holding fast to the principles that have served us well.

I began to sense that God was broadening my own vision shortly after Soul Survivor – The Message 2000. It had been an amazing summer of exciting and fruitful mission, all soaked in prayer and enabled by the selfless, unified involvement of hundreds of churches in and around Manchester.

Thousands of unchurched people had been positively affected by the gospel message, many hundreds of teenagers making initial commitments to Christ and immediately joining a church that had made meaningful contact with them through a local outreach project.

The highlight for me had been the impact made by the teams of young people that had worked on the many community projects, not only demonstrating the love of God in palpable ways but also bridging the gap between church and world in a relaxed, authentic and enjoyable manner.

The innumerable answers to prayer we saw in that year alone made me feel both privileged to be involved and humbled by the sheer magnitude of what our incredible God is able to do through his people when they come together in prayer for a city.

When we look back now to how things were in our city just a decade or so ago, we can see how much the spiritual atmosphere has been transformed. It really is rewarding for me to have played a part in what God is doing in Manchester, and to hear of similar examples in other towns and cities across the UK and beyond.

New wineskins

During the months following SSM2K, God began to prompt me to think of how to develop further the existing links between churches and how to build on the trust and respect that now bound so many together.

My sense was that he was challenging me to refocus my energies away from the familiar patterns of Prayer Network and to be ready to move into some new and uncharted waters.

I must confess that I found this very difficult to consider; it felt as though I was being asked to let go of everything I'd worked so hard for, and the timing seemed wrong because it was all going so well. Looking back, though, it's easy now to see that God doesn't make mistakes.

178

We can all desire to cling on tightly to things that may have actually served their purpose and run their course, while God is wanting to move us into a new phase of service that will require different methods and fresh relationships. Jesus talked about new wine needing new wineskins, the reason being that old ones harden with age and would simply burst if filled with newly produced wine that needs flexible containers in which to mature.

Actually, it was Frank who first suggested that maybe I ought to step back from Prayer Network and seek the Lord for guidance about the future. It took almost a year before I was able to see the rightness of this, eventually handing on the reins to Marijke Hoek, a key member of the core group, who had been with us from the start. She took on the leadership of the central Manchester borough and I retained my links with the groups in the other nine boroughs of Greater Manchester.

I felt that God was leading me into a new phase of networking that would mean both building on the existing foundations in and around Manchester and broadening out to link with other cities where God was doing similar things. To do this would require a totally new structure for me to work within; I really sensed that God was calling me to establish a new charitable trust that could start from scratch to respond to the new challenges he was setting before me.

However, such a step would take time, and I would need patience and wisdom to allow God to put the pieces together in his way and in his time. I knew it was right to let go of my formal role as the leader of Prayer Network, but I didn't know what I would do next. It was a very uncomfortable experience for me, just waiting on God and being still. Fortunately, though, it didn't last long at all!

The next big thing

Around this time, Andy Hawthorne was beginning to talk about Festival Manchester, another huge mission that would combine prayer, proclamation and presence in the style of SSM2K.

The plan, this time, was to partner with the Luis Palau Evangelistic Association, an international ministry that was pioneering a new approach to big missions. Andy had been invited to visit the USA for a firsthand look at this novel method, which involved hundreds of local churches co-operating to host a city-wide weekend of outdoor family entertainment interspersed with short, punchy gospel preaching from the main stage. He returned full of enthusiasm and absolutely convinced that God was opening a door for something similar in Manchester, especially given the existing network of praying churches and the recent success of SSM2K.

As it happened, Luis was keen to export his new model to Europe and he believed that God was indeed highlighting Manchester. Everyone was very excited and faith levels were high, despite the enormous budgets involved and the potential difficulties of transplanting a North American style event into a Northern European context: a challenge that had defeated many others in years gone by.

I was also invited to visit a Luis Palau Festival, this time in Santa Cruz, California, and came back with the same conviction that God was in this and we could do it. In no time at all, everything was agreed and the church in Manchester was gearing up for yet another enormous mission enterprise.

I was asked to work full time for a year on the Festival Manchester staff with the task of recruiting and co-ordinating 500 partner churches, and to plan the overall prayer strategy for the event. In many ways, this was the ideal role for me: I already knew the leaders of most churches in Greater Manchester, and my existing links with The Message were strong.

It was a one-off project that would keep me incredibly busy for the next twelve months and allow me time to pray and think about the future. The chance to do some similar things we had done for SSM2K but with the benefit of hindsight and a longer lead time was also very appealing, even if the challenge of increasing from 200 to 500 partner churches was a little daunting, to say the least!

Hitting targets

The ramp-up year for Festival was even more exciting than SSM2K, with loads of inter-church meetings happening in every borough and churches signing up to be involved on almost a daily basis.

As ever, one of the main items on the prayer agenda was finance: the budget this time was £1.8M (that was the original budget; after some cut-backs, we actually spent just over £1.5M)! Some of it would come from business sponsors, like Shell, Friends Provident, KPMG and others, but the majority came in gifts from generous Christians moved by God's Spirit: £40,000 was given by the 5,000 young delegates in a special offering taken at the main event – an awesome amount, especially when you consider that each one had already paid for the privilege of coming to Manchester to serve as a missionary!

Again, the police and local authorities were actively involved and very supportive. Many communities were positively impacted with the gospel in word and deed through the 320 outreach projects that took place all around the city. Once again, crime rates fell dramatically in some areas.

On the very last day before the mission week began, I surveyed my list of partner churches. Much to my amazement, and definitely as a result of loads of prayer, the count stood at 499, just one short of our target! I searched all my records to see if I could find just one more church that hadn't already registered but to no avail.

I was slightly disappointed because we'd prayed so hard in faith for 500, but I accepted that this was still an exceptional achievement and testimony to the many years of prayer and networking that had gone before.

Andy Hawthorne dropped into the Festival Office on that final afternoon as close of play approached. He knew that I really wanted to complete my target, and we laughed together about the idea of making up a fictitious church name just for the records! The Holy Mancunian United Apostolic Church of all Angels was his suggestion, but I resisted the temptation and began to prepare to leave the office for the very last time.

As I was filing away some papers, the phone rang. It was only a few minutes before 5.30 pm, and I thought about ignoring it. Instead, I answered and found myself responding to a few straightforward questions about arrival times and so on. The caller was the minister of Brown Lane Methodist Church, a name that didn't ring any bells at all.

A thought dawned, and I asked if the church had registered as a partner church; the minister said he couldn't remember whether he'd sent the form through. I checked my list and found they hadn't! 'You've just made my day!' I exclaimed, 'Have you got a fax machine nearby ...' Five minutes later, the official target was finally reached! Hallelujah! Another massive answer to prayer! There were 500 churches from every type of denomination and tradition all working together to see the city changed for Jesus. What a difference from the broken-down walls of ten years ago.

Prayer soaking

The format of Festival Manchester was slightly different from SSM2K. The plan was that, when the mission itself began, there would be three separate areas of activity through the week (Hot Zones), each one hosted by its own team of leaders; these would be responsible for worship, teaching and ministry in the mornings, local outreach projects in the afternoon and evangelistic evening meetings, with bands and gospel preaching.

We knew we would have to spread the prayer load far and wide and so I began to contact everyone I knew that had any prayer experience and ask them to stand with us. We formed prayer teams of 40 to 50 local people in each Hot Zone area and met regularly to pray there throughout the year. These were great occasions because so many people from the different churches already knew each other and didn't have to go through the learning curve of starting to work together across the varying traditions. We just got straight into praying; respecting and celebrating our different styles and enjoying the sense of God's approval of our unity of purpose and heart.

Two church leaders, David Baker and Adrian Glasspole, had the idea of doing a prayer drive around the M60 for the 40 days leading up to the Festival. It was a great way of surrounding the whole area with prayer and an easy thing to involve plenty of people in.

We met at the same time each evening in the Sainsbury's car park opposite Heaton Park, right next to the motorway junction. The final sections of the M60 had just been completed and, for the first time ever, it was now possible to drive in an unbroken circle around the whole of Greater Manchester.

As the Festival approached, the numbers of cars gradually increased, until there were dozens of cars packed with people prayer-driving the circular route. It was brilliant to see all the FM car stickers as we drove around. Some travelled clockwise, others anti-clockwise and there was much sounding of horns when we spotted one another passing on the opposite carriageway! Here's some feedback from Adrian:

> We drove just over 1,500 miles around the M60.
>
> Approx. 40 days @ approx. 36 miles = 1,440.
>
> Approx. 1,500 people responded to the good news of Jesus during Festival! Maybe it's a coincidence?
>
> Some evenings, there were just 2 people in just 1 car; once or twice it was myself – a Jewish believer – and Gudrun – a German Gentile! We have been in the front line of a vitally important battle. We have had 6 tyres slashed and various threats made – explicitly because we are believers! Yet the guy responsible was at Heaton Park on the Sunday. We prayed that we would be able to pray with 5 Jewish people; we prayed with 5 Jewish people. The rabbis in 2 synagogues we know of mentioned Festival in their Saturday morning services. They said that what the Christians had done was commendable, and that Jewish young people should aim to emulate their actions. But they went on to warn their flocks to avoid Heaton Park on Saturday and Sunday, as we would try to convert them! As we were praying on Sunday afternoon, one of the medics said we should pray for people to come to the Response Tent for healing. Before we had finished praying, a young man came in. He said God had told him to ask for prayer, as he had a bad leg. Not only did God heal him, but it turns out he was a Jewish believer! Our God is an AWESOME God!

One guy, Cyprian Yobera, an Anglican curate who'd moved from Kenya to serve as a member of the Eden team in

Harpurhey, decided to make his own prayer pilgrimage. He didn't need a car though, preferring to travel in the traditional Kenyan way: he ran every day from his home to Heaton Park and back for the same 40-day period. The return distance is about 12 miles, so he completed around 480 miles of prayer-running!

To make sure we could mobilise as much prayer as possible during the mission week itself, we came up with the idea of using a text message service to mobile phones. It proved to be an excellent way of circulating urgent requests to the prayer teams, especially when people were out on projects and not near a computer, and it came into its own on the second evening of the mission week.

Andy phoned me at midnight to ask me to get people praying as soon as possible. There'd been a lot of trouble that night at the Apollo, one of the Hot Zone venues; bricks had been thrown through buses transporting delegates, and rowdy crowds outside were doing their best to disrupt the evangelistic programme. Two young people had been taken to hospital with cuts and bruises. On top of this, there'd been no responses at all to the appeals in that particular Hot Zone, which was very unusual and an obvious sign of spiritual warfare.

I sent the text message out to the members of all the prayer teams, and we gathered for a special time of prayer in an upstairs room at the Apollo the next evening. We prayed fervently for the Holy Spirit to come upon the meeting that was going on below. We prayed for protection against violence and for a breakthrough in terms of serious decisions for Christ.

It was a powerful time and we were all full of faith, very much helped by the presence of some inspiring Ugandan intercessors, who prayed as though their lives depended on it!

At one point we all fell silent as we sensed the presence of God descending on the whole venue. From our removed position in a small room tucked away in the rafters of the ancient theatre, we didn't know that at that very moment the preacher in the main auditorium was giving an appeal that included a call for people to come forward and give their lives to Christ. All of a sudden, the quietness was broken as an almighty cheer erupted far below. The corporate roar of 2,000 young people reached our ears like the sound of a distant Alpine avalanche. Almost 200 people had responded!

The final statistics were a real encouragement to everyone, especially those who prayed earnestly for many young people to be converted. Here's a snippet from the final report: '... the three Hot Zones were attended by over 3,000 people each night, around half of these were unchurched people ... around 1,400 decisions for Christ, with more than half of these as first-time decisions'. Hallelujah!

Family focus

At the end of the week of youth activities, the climax of Festival was a weekend of family fun in Heaton Park, right next to tent-city, which once again became home to thousands of imported young missionaries from over 30 nations.

As well as appealing to the usual Message constituency of teenagers, the family weekend also attracted adults and chil-dren. There was an enormous, custom-built skate park that took hundreds of volunteers a few long days to construct. A group of professional Christian skaters came over from the States and performed amazing stunts interspersed with punchy testimonies through a PA system.

The impact was powerful. There was a constant crowd watching throughout the weekend, and hundreds of young people responded to gospel appeals. They were prayed with by the response team, who put them in touch with a partner church right away. The actual number of first-time decisions for Christ on the skate park alone was 230 over both days, more than at any festival in the USA.

Police estimated around 55,000 people visited the Festival in total. There were food stalls, puppet shows, stilt walkers, an exhibition of high-powered cars and all kinds of sideshows that kept everyone amused throughout the weekend. The Tribe and other major Christian artists rocked the park from the main stage until late into the evening on both days, and Luis and Andy popped up repeatedly with short bursts of gospel preaching, followed by appeals and more work for the busy counsellors in the response tent.

Wonderful! Exhilarating! And absolutely exhausting! I could have slept for a week if it wasn't for the adrenaline whizzing round my system. It's difficult to describe just how rewarding it felt to have been involved in such a breathtaking venture. At the same time, though, I have to confess that I could happily wait another few years before doing it all again!

City Links

During my year on the Festival Manchester staff I'd been putting the pieces in place for the launch of City Links, the new charitable trust that would enable me to continue networking people and churches for prayer and mission, not just in Manchester but also in other towns and cities, especially in the north-west.

I still didn't know exactly what I would be doing but I knew it would include organising large prayer gatherings and stirring Christians to pray and work in unity together for their region.

Because I strongly believe that ministry must be accountable within the body of Christ, I asked five people from around the UK to consider forming a council of reference: Jane Holloway of the Evangelical Alliance, Pete Greig of 24/7 Prayer, Russell Rook of the Salvation Army, Nic Harding of Frontline Church in Liverpool and Andy Hawthorne. I also asked three people from the north-west to consider becoming trustees: Robert Varnam and Julia Robertson from Manchester and Andy Prosser from Preston.

Within a few days, they'd all agreed, each one adding that they had a real sense of God's approval. We launched the new trust at the end of the big Festival Manchester prayer meeting at the Apollo in July 2003. I was prayed for and commissioned in my new role by Andy Hawthorne, Rob White (then senior pastor of Poynton Baptist Church) and Chick Yuill, a senior officer in the Salvation Army, and after the meeting finished there was a queue of people at the City Links stand signing up to become prayer partners. Again, a humbling and yet uplifting experience to sense God showing his approval through the tangible support and partnership of his people.

Redeeming the arts

God had been speaking to me for some time about gathering artists together for prayer and encouragement, and so I decided to make this the theme of the first City Links prayer event in February 2004.

The idea came from a prophecy we received from Rich Wilson a couple of years previously. With his wife, Ness, Rich co-leads the Open Heaven church in Loughborough. When he visited Manchester for a student celebration, he said he believed that Manchester, as a city, had a special call and gifting from God to excel in the arts. He reflected back to the

188

Hacienda nightclub, as one example among many, which was known throughout the world for its pioneering role in cutting-edge contemporary music. Rich went on to prophesy that God wanted to redeem the arts in Manchester and to raise up artists who would allow the Holy Spirit to use their art inside and outside the church for the extension of his kingdom.

Following this prophetic word, we'd featured the arts on two occasions. The first was as a theme for one of our regular Prayer Network meetings in September 2000, which was a first step to introducing the issue to the wider Christian community. We called that evening Art In Heaven, and we prayed for a wide range of people and ministries including musicians, singers, dancers, actors, painters, DJs and so on. Emma Varnam, then curator of a local authority art gallery, remembers the evening being particularly encouraging because of the diversity of age and art: 'It was wonderful to be in the company of so many gifted artists, all dedicated to their specific area of work and all committed to Christ,' she recalls.

The leader of an all-age dance and drama group called Caterpillar, said, 'To be prayed for and appreciated by hundreds of believers was a humbling and yet very encouraging experience for all of us, especially the young kids who really enjoyed being part of such a big occasion.' At the end of the evening, it was great to see rappers chatting away to classical musicians and poets getting to know dramatists, all enjoying the opportunity to network and make new friends.

As I mentioned earlier, we featured the arts again at our annual gathering in the summer of 2002 at the Lowry Theatre. This was a tremendous evening of praise and prayer and included an art exhibition that showcased a diverse range of artistic creativity. The Rhema Theatre Company performed a short play about Noah and the Ark on the concourse of the theatre for the benefit of passers-by. God even supplied a rainbow for the duration of the performance and kept the rain a mile or two in the distance until they had finished! Wellspring, the Manchester-based Christian orchestra, provided a jazz ensemble in each of the theatre's bars and a dozen or so painters and sculptors displayed their creations in the foyer: a few even managed to sell some of their work and gain new commissions; one has since been featured on television.

We consciously chose to include some non-Christian artists, friends of one of our organising group, because we felt God wanted us to demonstrate the inherent goodness of art, and because involving non-Christians had always seemed to be an important element of our approach to praying for the city. They provided us with some spectacular one-hundred-foot-high inflatables, giant brightly coloured fingers filled with com- pressed air, which wobbled and waved in the wind outside the theatre, announcing our presence to the world. The evening was a great success. Many people stayed afterwards to chat to the artists, appreciate their displays of creative work and enjoy a drink at the bars (which remained open until midnight – quite an unusual feature for a prayer meeting).

Building on the growing networks of artists that had come about as a result of these two events, we launched Redeeming the Arts in February 2004 as the first City Links prayer gather- ing. It was a tremendous occasion attended by over 400, mainly from the north-west but also from other parts of the UK, including Bristol, Birmingham, Leeds and London. Lloyd Gor- don, a bassist who regularly appears on TV as part of session bands for guest artists, spoke of the many temptations faced by Christians who work in the secular media. We prayed for protection for them, using him as a symbol and a representative of the many Christian musicians faithfully using their gifts on

190

this front line of enemy activity. Tina Cooke, a former presenter of *Blue Peter*, made the long trip from the capital, along with Steve Cole from Artisan, a Christian group reaching out to artists and media people in London. Tina explained the challenges involved in her work and encouraged us all to pray that God would raise up more Christians to work in broadcasting and to pray for their protection.

We also prayed that Christians in the media would gain more opportunities to influence the content and direction of programmes and films. This is a major area of spiritual warfare where very little ground is ever taken for the Lord. Sue Mayo, a former producer of *Brookside*, explained how difficult it is to be a Christian witness in that environment. Even though she held a position of influence for seven years she was never able to introduce a kingdom theme in the story-line, despite suggesting many credible ideas. One huge exception to this general rule was the film *The Passion of the Christ,* which was just about to be released in the UK. Nancy Goudie, from New Generations Ministries, showed us an advance excerpt and testified to the major impact even that short clip had made on her and her colleagues. We prayed that many would be moved to repentance and faith in the coming months as they watched the film.

One very common prayer request we kept on receiving from Christian artists was that they might be able to develop links with other like-minded people for support and encouragement. We prayed that this would happen increasingly through this new initiative. After this event, an arts therapist contacted us to say that she had met someone else in the same line of work and that they had immediately hit it off. She was really excited as she felt quite isolated in her work and frequently misunderstood, especially by other Christians, who sometimes suggested that her work was not particularly important to God.

Often, our prayers for artists are answered in very practical ways. A lady who is a visual artist had been painting for years but had always struggled to get her work displayed in the right places. Someone saw her paintings at the first Redeeming the Arts meeting and immediately offered to help her sell them. A singer, who was writing excellent crossover songs and going around the pubs with her work, sang for us at the celebration and has since been inundated with bookings.

It's well known that the artistic temperament is often sensitive and fragile and in need of regular affirmation. Sadly, we discovered that, in general, the church seems to be not particularly good at providing this. In many cases, artists tell us that their work is under-appreciated unless it deals with overtly religious themes and/or is used as part of a liturgical form. Yet many artists feel called by God simply to use their gifts in the world, and they believe that this in itself brings him glory. Part of the Redeeming the Arts vision is to show to the church the intrinsic value of art in general and to challenge Christians to respect and support artists in their calling. Our website offers opportunity for artists to advertise themselves and receive prayer and practical support. Currently, over 40 artists and groups are represented and the list is growing steadily.

Redeeming our communities

The redemption theme we chose for our arts focus fitted perfectly when we began to hear God speaking about developing our community outreach partnerships between churches, mission agencies, the police and local authorities.

To redeem something is to restore it to its initial condition, to get something back that was lost. In the ancient Greek of the New Testament, the word has strong connotations of the slave market, where people could literally be bought out of their condition of bondage at a price paid by someone else. This is one of the images that helps us understand the atoning work of Christ on the cross. In his death, our life is bought back. We are redeemed, rescued from our slavery to sin and restored to our original state of right relationship with God.

In the same way, God is at work through his church to redeem society. His ultimate goal is the redemption of the whole of the creation, including the spheres of work, leisure, art, family life, social relationships and so on.

Paul sets outs this cosmic plan of salvation most clearly in Colossians 1:16–20, where the repeated phrase 'all things' means exactly what it says. He is reconciling everything together in Christ. Our communities, damaged though they are by the effects of human selfishness, are nevertheless objects of God's love and targets for his power. They can be transformed when the life of God is channelled through the church in prayer and action. God not only wants to redeem individuals but communities as well. To turn them round and restore them as places of safety and nurture. To transform socially challenged areas into places of blessing. To change high-crime trouble spots into low-crime locations.

God challenged us to make sure that the excellent work done in many localities through SSM2K and Festival Manchester is not allowed just to stand as a memory of the past: we needed to maintain the momentum, strengthen the relationships and build on the foundations of trust and credibility that had been laid in such powerful and fruitful ways. So, we coined the phrase Redeeming Our Communities to summarise a whole new initiative that would combine prayer, networking, partnering and acting into a concerted drive that would start by praying specifically for the reduction of crime in certain areas, and spread out through new relationships between Christians and others into practical and powerful action to address the root causes of crime and suffering.

Common language

Amazingly, the same phrase, redeeming communities, recently began to appear in Government reports and on the lips of politicians and police chiefs; everyone was talking about redemption! We heard a senior member of cabinet quoted as saying, 'I believe in community redemption: I have to, I'm a Labour politician.' How exciting! The people with secular power are using the same language as those with divine power!

Targeting the north-west, we launched this new initiative with a large prayer celebration in September 2004 in the conference centre of the Reebok Stadium in Bolton, home of the Premier League football team, Bolton Wanderers. Senior police officers, chief executives of city councils, MPs, mayors and business leaders attended, along with well over 1,000 Christians from around the region.

Hazel Blears, a senior member of the Government, addressed the audience and spoke passionately about her own desire to see communities transformed. Again, the common language was amazing, although a theologically astute observer would be able to spot the subtle difference between her humanistic analysis, which emphasised social and political empowerment as the solution, and that of the Bishop of Bolton, whose prayer showed that he saw the gospel as the key! Even so, it's very exciting indeed that secular and Christian agendas are coming so closely into line with each other that the will to co-operate is outweighing the differences in philosophy.

As ever, we interviewed a number of people involved in different projects, such as Les Isaacs of Ascension Trust, who

194

is pioneering Street Pastors, a radical new approach to the problem of street crime in inner cities. Described by the BBC as 'a confrontational form of social work with a Christian flavour', Street Pastors trains young volunteers to go out late at night in the toughest areas of Manchester, Birmingham and London and get into conversation with the many youngsters that hang around: those most at risk of gang membership, drugs and guns. The volunteers dress in distinctive blue jackets and baseball caps with the Street Pastors logo clearly displayed. Perhaps surprisingly, most are female and not one of them has ever been assaulted. We prayed for God's power and strength to guard them, and for his Spirit to guide them as they seek to make connections into the lives of vulnerable young people, building bridges for Jesus one day to walk across.

We heard from senior police officers about how crime was significantly falling in areas where Christians were committed to ongoing prayer, and we were challenged to beware of complacency after big events like Festival Manchester: wonderful as it is to hear the statistics that prove the link between prayer and social order, we can't afford to make the mistake of assuming the effect is long term. The challenge to churches everywhere is to stay in touch with the police and to sustain concerted levels of prayer.

At the end of the evening, Christians were urged to start local prayer cells that would focus specifically on crime reduction in their own local area. As part of a continuing drive over the coming year, City Links will co-ordinate and resource these and connect with different police forces to provide up-to-date information and mutual encouragement.

The plan is to hold a similar gathering a year on and present the statistics that will, hopefully, show that prayer has a significant impact in crime reduction over a sustained period, not just during a ten-day mission. I feel a bit like Elijah must have felt when he challenged the prophets of Baal to see whose God was most powerful: a little scared but actually, deep down, highly confident that our God will be glorified!

Much appreciated

Here are some quotes I received after the launch evening:

I was greatly impressed by the whole occasion and the various presentations and it was no less than inspirational. There was an extremely powerful message connecting religion and faith with personal responsibility and community action and with the critical role the police play in our communities. I wish the project every success.

Robert Hough, High Sheriff of Greater Manchester

I am always pleased to develop partnerships with those who have a long-term commitment to work in and for our communities … Together we really can Make A Difference and I applaud your commitment and efforts.

Michael Todd, Chief Constable, Greater Manchester Police

What a fantastic night! We got loads of ideas for Lancashire and our church. You and your team did a great job.

Chris Gradwell, Community Beat Manager
Co-ordinator, Lancashire Police

We want to send you our wholehearted encouragement as you launch this pioneering initiative of partnership between police, churches and the communities across

196

the North West of England founded on prayer ... [hope-
fully it will] be a transferable model to other cities across
the UK and beyond.

Evangelical Alliance: Malcolm Duncan 'Head of Mission',
Jane Holloway 'Prayer & Evangelism', Julia Wensley
'Social Responsibility'

We should have more evenings like this!

Hazel Blears, MP for Salford

I enjoyed the evening and subsequently I intend to ensure
that Sefton plays a very positive role in Merseyfest 2005.

Graham Haywood, Chief Executive,
Sefton Council, Merseyside

Sustaining the impact

We said at the start of the book that it all begins with prayer but
that shouldn't imply that prayer is simply a stage through which
we pass on the way to action.

Many Christians seem to hold the view that once something
has been prayed for it can be 'left with the Lord', which may well
be true of things such as personal sins for which forgiveness is
being sought but simply can't be the case when it comes to
praying for a city to be changed. We have to pray continually,
believing that God is hearing, answering and guiding our
prayers in line with his own agenda.

Not only does everything begin with prayer but it's prayer that
keeps it going. Prayer is not a prelude to activity; if we're going
to start to pray that God would bring lasting change to our city,
we'll need to be prepared to keep on praying. If we see
answers, such as falling crime rates, that should spur us on to

continue rather than suggest that we've done the job. When Jesus spoke in parables about prayer he often made the point that prevailing prayer is persistent prayer. Scholars point out that when Jesus said 'Ask and it will be given to you' in Matthew 7:7, the original Greek is in the continuous sense and can be translated 'ask and keep on asking'. Paul urges Christians to 'pray continually' (1 Thessalonians 5:17).

The renewal of interest in spiritual warfare during the latter part of the twentieth century has helpfully reminded us that our prayers are actually weapons that play a key role in the heavenly battle between the forces of good and evil in the unseen realm. When numbers of Christians agree together on earth that they want to see their community transformed to the point that they are prepared to put aside their differences and seek the Lord together in prayer, something changes in the spiritual realm. Some sort of initial breakthrough occurs as the church of Christ takes the initiative against the gates of hell, which cannot prevail against a militant army of unified believers. But we would be immediately surrendering back whatever ground we'd taken if we simply stopped and declared the victory won. Likewise, if we merely repeated the same manoeuvre over and over again, the best we could expect would be to stand still and at worst we would be shadow-boxing.

So, it all begins with prayer and it all continues with prayer. But, to keep the whole thing in balance we need to remind ourselves that it would also be a serious mistake to remain so focused on the spiritual activity of prayer that we never allowed God to stir us into practical action. Prayer is about God grabbing our attention as well as us gaining his! Jim Graham says, 'Prayer is not so much about us getting God on our side to solve the problems in our lives as him getting us on his side to serve his purposes in the world.'

The fact that we've seen specific answers when we've prayed that crime rates would fall in our city is extremely encouraging, but the actual crimes themselves are only the surface issue. We need to press on, seeking God for revelation about the underlying factors that are at work in a high-crime community. God may be just as concerned about the causes of crime as the criminal acts themselves.

We can build the spiritual walls higher by researching the social, economic and educational infrastructure of the area and praying further into what we find. There may be more we can do through our newly developed networks across churches and mission agencies to begin to campaign and to act for change, and to communicate the gospel creatively in word and deed.

Imagine how powerful the church in our land could become if we fused together all the many strengths of its various expressions: prophetic voices speaking loudly and clearly to the nation about the need for justice; intercessors persistently knocking on heaven's door, crying out for power for the church; activists serving on the front line; evangelists declaring the biblical truth of salvation; entrepreneurs creating projects to break the generational cycle of unemployment; pastors helping new believers to find their place in the family of God, and counsellors and carers helping to set free the victims of addiction and abuse. Praying for a city to be changed begins to look a whole lot more challenging!

Some of this is already happening in Manchester, and we can see already the fulfilment of some of the long-term element of the vision God gave us initially. As the spiritual walls of our city are being rebuilt through unity and prayer, so new 'towers' are appearing within the newly strengthened spiritual environment. New church plants are thriving; new ministries are emerging; new partnerships are forming.

One exciting example is that of Youth For Christ and The Message, who have joined forces to work together in the youth sections of the prisons in Greater Manchester. They are jointly funding a full-time team in each of the six young offenders' institutions to run Alpha courses for inmates. They will also work with newly released prisoners to provide them with halfway-house accommodation, train them for work and help them integrate into one of the Eden Partnerships around the city. They will create businesses that can be run by ex-offenders, and each prison will eventually be linked to a fully funded Life Centre that will offer all these services as part of a joined-up approach to holistic mission.

Another example is Projects Skate Park, which is now up and running in Manchester city centre. The ramps were left over at the end of Festival Manchester and, after much prayer and negotiation, a miracle occurred that nobody would have dared to even dream about a few years ago. The city council, for decades vehemently opposed to all things Christian, gave permission for a group of funky young Christian skaters to set up underneath a section of the Mancunian Way and run a skate park that not only provides a safe and affordable place for kids to skate but also a dynamic evangelistic environment and paid employment for young urban missionaries!

It's quite remarkable to witness the turnaround in the attitudes of secular authorities towards the church. After years of being marginalised at best, ignored or abused at worst, suddenly Christians are now appreciated and valued, even treated with respect! It has everything to do with prayer and a lot to do with the subsequent realisation that the church and the state do share some common goals: to see our cities changed and our society improved. The secular world is beginning to see that social change is the normal business of the church.

One voice

Looking back over a decade and more of city-reaching ministry has been a wonderfully uplifting experience for us. We've spent hours sifting through back issues of 'Update', the information sheet we produced for our Prayer Network evenings, some examples of which are available online at www.citylinks.org.uk .

We've had to cast our minds back to times and people we'd completely lost touch with and, in so doing, have been really encouraged by the reminders of how God is working so powerfully in so many challenging settings

We've realised how much we take for granted the 'new thing' that God is doing in drawing Christians together for prayer and action. We've grown so used to our large, inter-church gatherings that we often forget just how unusual they are. The same is true of our leaders' gatherings, where denominational allegiances take a back seat and warm smiles and godly hugs are the order of the day.

One small but lasting example of what God has been doing in our city is the 'unity sign' that now adorns the buildings of hundreds of churches all across the UK. The story behind this began in 1999, when an Anglican church in a little corner of Greater Manchester contacted a local sign-writer to order a large, oval sign that proclaimed the lordship of Christ in the context of all the interest in the imminent Millennium. In big, bold, white lettering on a tasteful, dark-green background, the message read, 'The Millennium is Christ's 2,000th birthday. Worship Him here today.'

In spite of the inevitable Christian nit-picking over the chronological accuracy of this claim, the sign was an instant hit and, within a few weeks, just about every church building in the diocese had found a prominent place to display one. Not just Anglican churches, too – Roman Catholics, Methodists, URCs,

Baptists, Pentecostals and so on, all were seen and heard to be speaking with one voice to the outside world. The idea spread rapidly around the city and, by the time the New Year's fireworks were exploding, nearly every single church building was wearing its own badge of one-voice oneness.

A couple of years later, Frank and I, along with Dennis Wrigley, the leader of the Maranatha Community, and Kevin McKenna, a Roman Catholic friend, approached the sign-writer and suggested that it might be a good idea to offer a new version, now that the new Millennium was well underway. They were very keen and asked us to suggest the wording. Frank came up with a paraphrase of Ephesians 4:4–6 that reads, 'One Church, one faith, one Lord: Jesus Christ. Worship Him here today.' Now most of the green ovals have given way to the new maroon version, but the message rings out just as clearly: the church of Christ is united. We all have our differences but our core message is the same, and we declare it with authority and conviction together. All are singing from the same hymn sheet for a change!

As we've stressed repeatedly throughout the book, though, there is still a long way to go. The degree of unity we are experiencing in Manchester is certainly impressive given the landscape of ten or so years ago, but there are still some unresolved issues and awkward tensions between a few groups and individuals. Our feeling is that this is the inevitable reality of human relationships. As Jesus reminds us, the weeds will always grow among the crops (Matthew 13:30). As long as we remain in our imperfect condition, there are bound to be misunderstandings and disagreements that arise. The challenge is for us to deal with them in a way that glorifies God, with maturity, respect, humility and honesty. 'Speaking the truth in love, we will in all things grow up into him who is the Head, that is, Christ' (Ephesians 4:15).

We feel tremendously honoured and privileged to be involved in this ministry of enabling united prayer in our city and elsewhere. It's been thrilling to see God working out his redemptive purposes not only in individual lives but also, through the one true church, in communities as well. 'Now to him who is able to do immeasurably more than all we ask or imagine, according to his power that is at work within us, to him be glory in the church and in Christ Jesus throughout all generations, for ever and ever! Amen' (Ephesians 3:20–21).

appendix
extra stuff to dip into

Paper on identificational repentance

Prepared for the Cornerstone Network Theological Forum, September 1999 by Frank N. Green, B.A. (Hons) Theol.M.A. (Bib. Studies). Also published on the Evangelical Alliance website:

The question set by the Forum was:

'Identificational repentance – Is it necessary? Is it biblical?'

Introduction

Identificational repentance is a term coined by John Dawson in *Healing America's Wounds*[1] to describe a type of prayer which identifies with and confesses before God the sins of one's nation, city, people group, church or family. It may also involve formally apologising to and asking the forgiveness of representatives of the victims of the corporate sins (such as white Christians repenting of racism and asking a representative group of black people for forgiveness in a public ceremony).

Dawson has worked closely with Cindy Jacobs, who for ten or more years has taught on healing the nations through a type of corporate prayer that urges the church to act in a priestly role by confessing and repenting of the corporate sins of the nations.

As a practice, identificational repentance has been encouraged in the context of mission, especially by those with a strong spiritual warfare slant to their ministry. They argue that the corporate sins of a nation or city form a major obstacle to the revival God wants to bring, and that when the church takes time to investigate and research the history of her nation/city, the Holy Spirit will reveal to her the specific roots of that which blocks the blessing. The next steps[2] are the same as those taken by an individual who turns to God but with the added dimension of the involvement of a group of intercessors:

1. Identify the national sin.
2. Confess the sin.
3. Apply Christ's blood.
4. Walk in obedience and repair the damage.

A great deal of anecdotal material[3] is cited in support of the methodology suggesting that major spiritual breakthrough has been achieved as a direct result of the employment of this and other 'new spiritual weapons'.[4]

Is it biblical?

The biblical references used to validate the practice of identificational repentance are from the Hebrew Bible. Mostly, these are examples of prophets who recognise that the nation of Israel has disobeyed God both in her immediate circumstances and in her history and is therefore reaping the consequences in terms of political, economic, moral and religious decay.

Two key texts, however, are almost always referred to as foundational to the practice of identificational repentance. They are 2 Chronicles 7:14, 'If my people, who are called by my name, will humble themselves and pray and seek my face and turn from their wicked ways, then will I hear from heaven and will forgive their sin and will heal their land'; and Exodus 20:5b, 'I, the Lord your God, am a jealous God, punishing the children for the sin of the fathers to the third and fourth generation of those who hate me.'

It is clear from the many examples cited by its proponents and practitioners that identificational repentance is certainly biblical. Overwhelmed by the presence of God in the Temple, Isaiah expresses his heartfelt repentance on behalf of the entire nation of Israel (Isaiah 6:5); faced with the terrible threat of national judgement, Jeremiah acknowledges the wickedness of his own generation and the guilt of his ancestors (Jeremiah 14:20); as he fasts and prays for Israel, Daniel repents of the sins of the nation (Daniel 9:20) and when he hears of the devastation of Jerusalem, Nehemiah also repents of the corporate sin of the people of God that has brought it about (Nehemiah 1:6). It seems quite clear to me that these men are repenting before God out of a genuine sense of responsibility for the state of their nation. They acknowledge that the problems began a long time ago but seem to admit that they and their own immediate contemporaries are equally guilty of disobeying the Lord in their own time. For me, this is identificational repentance: people of God identifying, under the conviction of the Holy Spirit, their own part in the corporate sin of their nation, city or people group. What I find puzzling is the consistent insistence by those seeking to validate the modern practice with these biblical examples that these prayers represent a type of symbolic identification with the sins of Israel rather than a personal confession of their direct responsibility as a part of the whole.

The distinction arises out of the treatment of Exodus 20:5, which refers to generational ties. There is a difference, they argue, between the sins of the fathers (these being original acts of rebellion towards God) and the iniquity (a different Hebrew word) with which the subsequent generations will be visited (this being the consequences of the original acts). This means that when Nehemiah, for example, acknowledges that both his 'father's house' and he have sinned, he is confessing the sins of his ancestors and the effect they have had upon him. And when Daniel says 'I was … confessing my sin and the sin of my people', he is doing the same. Neither, apparently, is confessing personal culpability; they are vicariously repenting on behalf of their ancestors.

This is foundational, since it gives a biblical precedent to those who want to identify with the sins committed by others perhaps thousands of years ago and offer their repentance to God (and maybe to the descendants of the original victims). I am not convinced by this interpretation. It seems to me that the identification we see in people like Nehemiah and Daniel is not substitutionary or vicarious but a recognition of personal culpability and a willingness to represent the nation in priestly prayer. They seem to me to be realising that their own attitudes and/or actions towards God, his laws and other people are no different from those of their ancestors. They are acknowledging that they stand in a line of continuity with previous generations who have sinned, and they are confessing the actual part they are playing in perpetuating the sin and its consequences. They are repenting of sin not in a symbolic way but in an honest act of self-surrender before God.

My assertion, then, is that identificational repentance is biblical but vicarious repentance is not.

This is important in terms of providing a biblical paradigm. It seems perfectly right to me for a group of praying Christians who come under a sense of conviction of the Spirit for the corporate sin of their nation towards another, or for the corporate sin of their people group towards another, then to acknowledge their part in the perpetuating of that sin and to repent towards God, asking for forgiveness, a breaking of the cycle and corporate healing in line with the promises of God in 2 Chronicles 7:14. This would be biblical, meaningful and powerful. God keeps his promises, and when the church acts in obedience and humility and admits its own sin in line with the sins of the nations, then forgiveness will flow and the land can be healed. What I cannot accept is the idea that Christians can symbolically repent on behalf of other people's sins without admitting their own guilt. Such an activity is meaningless, misleading and out of line with the biblical teaching that each person is responsible for their own sin and will be judged accordingly.

At a conference in Newcastle, County Down in January 1998, a gathering of prayer leaders from the UK and Ireland listened as the history of the Northern Ireland 'Troubles' was explained. The root was identified as the seventeenth-century 'Plantation' of Scottish and English Protestants into Ulster by the Government, who authorised them to dispossess Catholics of their land and property, killing them if they offered resistance. Those organising the conference asked the Scottish and English delegates to stand and acknowledge to God on behalf of their seventeenth-century countrymen and women that what had taken place was sinful. The Irish delegates were asked to express forgiveness to the Scots and English, who were confessing sins for which they were not personally responsible. Those who took part, including Debra and I, felt they had

209

participated in something meaningful and helpful. We recognised that, although we had not been responsible for the original evil actions that set the hostilities in motion 300 years ago, nevertheless we shared a sense of responsibility for the current situation. Our personal sectarianism and inherent racism was exposed. We knew we were guilty, and that our guilt was part of something bigger that was affecting the whole nation. So our identificational repentance was appropriate and relevant at both the personal and the corporate levels. How effective it was in terms of bringing healing to the land is, of course, impossible to measure.

Is it necessary?

We must be careful in trying to answer this question. We British find it far too easy to dismiss things that originate in other parts of the world, and we are inherently conservative in our theology and practice. If this is part of the 'new thing' God is doing then we need to be open to it and to embrace it wholeheartedly.

The practice of identificational repentance has much to commend it. It has the potential to reorientate the church in the West in the following ways:

- It moves us away from our comfortable, self-seeking inwardness. The original setting from which this concept emerged has a strong missions thrust. It is prayer for the nation/city. Prayer with an outward focus. Prayer for other people rather than for ourselves. Sadly, some of its practitioners have turned it into yet another item for internal consumption on the conference calendar but that does not alter its inherently evangelistic nature.

- It moves us away from 'arm's length' evangelism to incarnational mission. A distant and aloof church can never identify with the nation of which it is a part. Only a church that is immersed in the culture of those it is trying to reach can properly engage in identificational repentance.

- It moves us away from the individualism that so often characterises Western spirituality. The whole concept is based on the corporate nature of a nation/city/people group and so we are forced to move away from individualism and isolated self-sufficiency towards community and interdependence. It is theoretically possible to practise identificational repentance alone but, realistically, it tends to occur in groups, which reinforces the point further.

- It moves us away from triumphalism. This is why it is so important that those doing the repenting are sincere and genuinely contrite. The church is a family of broken people who are aware of their sinfulness. When the church admits its own failure in solidarity with the rest of the human race and asks for forgiveness from those she has offended (as in the case of the Reconciliation Walk)[5] the world will begin to listen more closely to her message.

Perhaps the real question being asked here is whether identificational repentance is necessary as a prelude to revival. Should everyone do it? Will revival be delayed in places that refuse to follow the format and implement the strategy?

It is dangerous to suggest that identificational repentance is 'the key' to revival for a number of reasons:

- There is no clear NT reference to it: Jesus never mentioned it, nor did Paul or any of the other NT authors (although, as we have seen, the Hebrew Bible contains numerous examples in the context of the nation of Israel before Jesus came, so it is not an unbiblical activity).

211

- The NT paradigms for church activity would suggest that they hold what keys there might be to revival, namely apostolic teaching, authority and church planting; prophetic, anointed preaching with signs and wonders following; caring for the poor and disenfranchised; daily worshipful living that wins the favour of outsiders and so on. Although none of these negates the promise of God in 2 Chronicles 7:14 that revival will only come through a penitent and humble church.

- Revival has occurred in many parts of the world throughout history without any conscious identificational repentance taking place, so unless God has shed some of his omnipotence or changed his *modus operandi* then we can be confident that he will continue to get his will done through his church one way or another.

If the Holy Spirit speaks to someone and directs them to repent on behalf of the corporate sins of their nation or people group then, of course it is necessary that they obey. This raises a number of questions:

- Do those present genuinely and readily identify with the specific corporate sin and the people group concerned? Can they personally admit to playing a part in the wider issue? Is it meaningful for them? If not, they ought to be excused from the activity and not coerced into taking part in something that would be, at best, a religious ritual.

- Has the 'revelation' been properly submitted to and tested by the appropriate level of leadership? Most of the material I have read on the subject refers at some point to an individual who 'felt' that a particular corporate sin was being revealed to them. There seems to me to be a lack of accountability around many of the groups that are practis-

212

ing identificational repentance. Some are splinter groups within churches where the leadership has backed away rather than exercise responsible authority. In the long term, this is bound to cause division and pain. Others are para-church groups which are self-validating and 'untouchable'; often these groups relate to a high-profile figure who themselves are independent from any recognised authority structures.

- Has there been clear teaching ahead of the issue? Often, in the context of ordinary church life, it is the very sugges-tion of the need for any type of spiritual warfare that prompts some sort of explanation from the leadership. Sometimes this may provide a good opportunity to bring some teaching on the subject. More often than not, how-ever, it causes some people to make hasty decisions either to accept or reject a particular position. This can be avoided by teaching through potentially contentious subjects in a systematic way within the life of the local church.

There are enough clear commands from Jesus and the NT writers for us to follow without shading off into peripheral activities in the search for revival.

Criticism has been levelled in recent years at those who became obsessed with narrow areas of activity, such as heal-ing, or deliverance, or speaking in tongues. Identificational repentance has the potential to dominate some people's lives in a similar way. It is certainly a valid activity but only in the context of the general mission of the church.

A number of further questions need to be asked:

- Is there a preoccupation with certain types of sin in some circles? The sociological analysis of the spiritual warfare movement frequently sounds like that of the US Moral Majority or the former Tory Government in the UK There seems to be a fascination with divorce and abortion statistics reflecting how the West is sliding into the abyss. I am not suggesting these are not accurate, just wondering whether the motivation may be one of wanting to return to the good old days of 'family values'. It is just possible that the subconscious agenda reflects the aspirations of the middle-aged, middle-class, mid-West or middle-England membership of the movement itself, rather than the 'now-word' of God himself.

- Is it easier to engage in repentance than mission? John Dawson says that we need to 'keep doing it until it's over'.[6] Isn't this playing directly into the hands of the enemy by busying ourselves with anything other than actually sharing good news with lost people, which is supposed to be the primary activity of the church militant.

- How do we know if or when we have 'broken through' and actually received the forgiveness for which we are asking? Will there be quantifiable results in the material realm that 'breakthrough' has occurred in the spiritual realm? Cindy Jacobs' suggestion that we 'keep on confessing until there is no more pain'[7] is a nice soundbite but difficult advice to follow.

- Perhaps this is the most serious question of all: is it easier to repent of other people's sins than those of our own? We Western Christians perhaps should devote more time to measuring our own lifestyles against the needs of the poor in our own present day than digging around in our ancestry looking for the root causes of their poverty. There may well be some railway-sleeper-sized sins sitting comfortably in the corner of our own eyes that require urgent attention before we start focusing on the specks of dust in our history.

214

1   John Dawson, *Healing America's Wounds*, Ventura: Regal Books, 1994.
2   C. Peter Wagner, 'The Power to Heal the Past' in *Renewal Journal No. 8: Awakening*, Brisbane: Renewal, 1996, pp. 14–18.
3   Gary S. Greig, *Healing the Land: What Does the Bible Say about Identificational Repentance, Prayer and Advancing God's Kingdom?* Unpublished paper for The International Reconciliation Coalition listing examples of prayer gatherings that led to 'amazing things happening in the heavenlies as a result' of the identificational repentance practised. For similar material, see also: C. Peter Wagner, *Wrestling With Dark Angels*, Ventura: Regal Books, 1990; Cindy Jacobs, *Possessing the Gates of the Enemy*, London: Marshall Pickering, 1993.
4   Wagner, 'The Power to Heal the Past', p. 14.
5   The Reconciliation Walk took place between Spring 1996 and Summer 1999. Led by Lynn Green, YWAM's European and Middle East Director, it involved 3,000 people in walking the routes of the 'Christian' Crusades of the Middle Ages, culminating in Jerusalem on the 15th July 1999, the 900th anniversary of one of the many Crusade massacres of Jews and Arabs. The purpose of the walk was to identify with and repent of the sins of those Christians responsible for the genocide that occurred in the name of Christianity. An apology was read personally to many Orthodox Christians, Muslims and Jews, stating that the Crusaders had 'betrayed the name of Christ by conducting themselves in a manner contrary to his wishes and character'. The walkers expressed their 'deep regret for the atrocities committed in the name of Christ by our predecessors'. More details in *Renewal* magazine, September 1999.
6   Wagner, 'The Power to Heal the Past', p. 16.
7   *Ibid.*

Survivor books . . . receive as you read!

Survivor Books came out of a desire to pass on revelation, knowledge, experience and lessons learnt by lead worshippers and teachers who minister to our generation.

We pray that you will be challenged, encouraged and inspired and receive as you read.

The Survivor Book Sampler: only £1
Sample all 21 Survivor books, including money off vouchers!

survivor

www.survivor.co.uk

God on the Beach: Michael Volland (£6.99)

Newquay: the UK's infamous summer party capital. The town heaving with young clubbers and surfers, each one desperate to live life to the full, eager for experience, ready to ride the waves and hit the heights. Into this caotic carnival dropped Michael Volland, DJ, surfer, and team member in a beach mission 21st century style. There was just one problem, Michael was not at all sure that God would turn up.

City-Changing Prayer: Debra & Frank Green (£6.99)

Imagine a regular city-wide gathering of Christians united and focused in prayer. Imagine a church that serves local institutions, and asks nothing in return. Imagine the crime rate falling; teenagers praying; people beginning to believe that there's something in this thing called prayer. Frank and Debra Green have seen all this and more over the past ten years. They have learnt lessons about how to foster mutual trust and spiritual fruitfulness, overcoming the obstacles both inside and outside the church family.

Diary of a Dangerous Vision: Andy Hawthorne (£6.99)

This is the story of Andy Hawthorne's dramatic conversion and the adventure of an ever-growing group of Christian's set to take Christ into the most tough urban areas. Reading this book will leave you challenged and inspired.

survivor

www.survivor.co.uk

Rad Lad Livin: Mark Bowness (£6.99)
The perfect manual to help any lad move forward in God, tackling issues ranging from lust to identity, from brotherhood to homosexuality – this book is practical in its nature and real in its content. Mark has grappled with biblical issues in order to present them in a real and relevant way, then sprinkled it with stories of past and present, making this a challenging, interesting and significant book for any lad to read.

Wasteland: Mike Pilavachi (£6.99)
With honesty and wit, Mike helps us to understand – and even relish – those difficult times in our lives when our dreams are unrealised and our spirituality feels dry and lifeless. Drawing from characters in the Old and New Testament, he puts together a biblical survival kit for the journey so that hope shimmers on the horizon like a distant oasis.

The Truth Will Set You Free: Beth Redman (£5.99)
With insight and humour, Beth helps young women to find God's answers to the big questions and struggles in their lives. Thousands of teenage girls have come to trust Beth Redman's powerful and relevant teaching through her packed seminars at Soul Survivor.

survivor

www.survivor.co.uk

Passion for Your Name: Tim Hughes (£6.99)

Timely and timeless advice for today's leader. If you want
to be more involved in leading worship in your church, or
become a more effective member of the band, then this
book is a great place to begin. Tim Hughes looks first at
the reasons why we worship God, and why we need to
get our hearts right with him, before moving on to the
practicalities of choosing a song list, musical dynamics,
small group worship, and the art of songwriting.

The Air I Breathe: Louie Giglio (£6.99)

For some it's the office. For others, the mirror. "When you
follow the trail of your time, energy affection, and money"
says Louie, "you find a throne. And whatever is on that
throne is the object of your worship!" Learn to give your
life to the only One worthy of it.

The Unquenchable Worshipper: Matt Redman (£5.99)

This book is about a kind of worshipper; unquenchable,
undivided, unpredictable. On a quest to bring glory and
pleasure to God, these worshippers will not allow
themselves to be distracted or defeated. Matt uses many
examples from the Bible and draws on his own experience as a worship leader, to show us how to make our
worship more meaningful.

survivor

www.survivor.co.uk

Facedown: Matt Redman (£5.99)

"When we face up to the glory of God, we soon find ourselves facedown in worship". Matt Redman takes us on a journey into wonder, reverence and mystery – urging us to recover the "otherness" of God in our worship.

Heart of Worship Files: Compiled by Matt Redman (£7.99)

A mixture of creative biblical insights and hands-on advice on how to lead worship and write congregational songs. Contributors include: Mike Pilavachi; Tim Hughes; Graham Kendrick; Darlene Zschech and Matt Redman. This book will encourage and inspire you to new heights of worship, giving practical advice for worship leaders, creative advice for musicians and perceptive insights into the theology of worship.

Inside Out Worship: Compiled by Matt Redman (£6.99)

Outside-in worship never works; true worship always works itself from the inside, out. A love for God, which burns on the inside and cannot help but express itself externally too. Purposeful lives of worship exploding from passionate and devoted hearts. Guidance from some of today's most seasoned leaders and lead worshippers, including Darlene Zschech, Robin Mark, Tim Hughes, Chris Tomlin, Brian Houston, Terl Bryant and many more.

survivor

www.survivor.co.uk

Red Moon Rising: Pete Greig (£7.99)

24-7 is at the centre of a prayer revival across the globe and this book gives a fantastic insight into what God is doing with ordinary prayer warriors. Read inspiring stories of people finding a new depth of heartfelt prayer and radical compassion.

The Vision & the Vow: Pete Greig (£6.99)

Has your faith become a chore where once it was a passion? Are you tired of the self-serving mentality of our culture? Join Pete Greig on the adventure of a lifetime in this inspiring and beautifully illustrated book; unlocking God's ultimate vision for your life and your community.

24-7 Prayer Manual (£9.99)

People are praying 24 hours a day, 7 days a week in countries around the world, with as a many as 20 prayer rooms running concurrently. This concise but detailed guide will help churches, youth groups, Christian Unions and groups of churches set up prayer rooms for one day, one week or one month. The book gives an introduction to the ethos of 24-7 and a step by step guide to setting up a prayer room. It's full of creative, low cost ideas that will help make the life changing prayer room experience accessible to everyone. Includes CD Rom.

survivor

www.survivor.co.uk

Salvation's Song: Marcus Green (£6.99)

Worship changes us. It changes our views of God, of the world, and of ourselves. . .at least it should. Marcus Green takes us on a journey through some of the big issues of Christian faith, making some exciting discoveries about the liberating nature of true worship. Jesus died so that we can worship God. That's the good news. That's the gospel.

The Shock of Your Life: Adrian Holloway (£6.99)

Dan, Becky and Emma have one thing in common. . .they just died. Were they ready? Do heaven and hell really exist? Are you a red-hot Christian? A lukewarm Christian? Or maybe you've never even considered Christianity. . .well, this book is for you. Read it for yourself and be shocked to the core.

Aftershock: Adrian Holloway (£6.99)

Dan is back. Back from the dead. Now there'll be trouble. Dan was the sole survivor of an accident that propelled three young people into the afterlife. Now he's back, ready to convince his friends and family that Jesus is their only hope before they face judgement after death. Adrian Holloway gives readers and youth leaders a powerful weapon in their spiritual armoury.

survivor

www.survivor.co.uk

Jesus Freaks II: DC Talk (£11.99)

Rarely has a book captured the attention of Christians of all ages as Jesus Freaks has with its stories of Christian martyrs. Featuring testimonies of revolutionaries who took a stand for Christ against the culture of their day, along with new stories of martyrs through the centuries. DC Talk challenge readers to pray for the persecuted church around the world and openly stand for Jesus.

Studentdom: Matt Stuart (£7.99)

In addition to study and exams the university years bring a new freedom, character development and the building of what may become lifelong friendships. But they can be daunting too, particularly for Christian students who may worry about fitting in or about misusing their new-found freedom. Matt Stuart provides a comprehensive guide to all aspects of university life, including areas such as relationships and debt management.

Prices are correct at the time of going to press but may change.

survivor

www.survivor.co.uk